THE AUTISM INCLUSION
TOOLKIT

THE AUTISM INCLUSION
TOOLKIT
Training Materials and Facilitator Notes

MAGGIE BOWEN AND LYNN PLIMLEY

Los Angeles • London • New Delhi • Singapore

First Published 2008

SAGE Publications Ltd
1 Oliver's Yard
55 City Road
London EC1Y 1SP

SAGE Publications Inc.
2455 Teller Road
Thousand Oaks, California 91320

SAGE Publications India Pvt Ltd
B 1/I 1 Mohan Cooperative Industrial Area
Mathura Road
New Delhi 110 044

SAGE Publications Asia-Pacific Pte Ltd
33 Pekin Street #02-01
Far East Square
Singapore 048763

Library of Congress Control Number: 2007936019

British Library Cataloguing in Publication data

A catalogue record for this book is available from
the British Library

ISBN 978-1-4129-4756-5
ISBN 978-1-4129-4757-2 (pbk)

Typeset by CEPHA Imaging Pvt. Ltd., Bangalore, India
Printed in Great Britain by The Cromwell Press Ltd, Trowbridge, Wiltshire
Printed on paper from sustainable resources

Contents

CD Contents

Key of Icons

1 Section objectives

2 Issues to consider

3 Extension activities

4 Recommended reading

5 Case studies

6 Go to the CD

7 Useful websites

8 Useful resources

Acknowledgements

We would like to thank participants on Autism Cymru's Inclusive Schools and ASDs: Whole School Training and Research Project and the School Forum members for continually providing us with best practice examples, Mike Ridout for his advice on Section 12 and NoMAD for endless enthusiasm and promotion. Many thanks to our Senior Commissioning Editor, Jude Bowen and the team at SAGE for all their support and encouragement during the production of this book.

About the Authors

MAGGIE BOWEN

Maggie gained her academic and professional qualifications at universities in Aberystwyth, Leeds and Bangor. She has trained as a team inspector of secondary and special schools and has worked as a Threshold Assessor in England. She is an affiliate member of the British Psychological Society and a Fellow of the Higher Education Academy.

Maggie began her teaching career in school for children with severe learning difficulties (SLD) in North Wales. She has also spent time in mainstream education and worked as a Community Liaison Teacher (CLT) for individuals with SLD. As a CLT, in addition to providing a link between home and school, she was a core member of a multi-agency team responsible for developing a range of new services for individuals of all ages with a SLD.

In 1991, Maggie took up the position of programme leader for Special Educational Needs (SEN) courses and the M.A. in Education at the North East Wales Institute (NEWI) of Higher Education in Wrexham. During her time at NEWI, she worked as a consultant/writer for ACCAC on their publication A *Structure for Success. The National Curriculum and Pupils with ASDs*. In 2000, Maggie was elected as the first President of NASEN (Wales). She has published on a range of SEN issues in books and journals and presented papers at conferences at home and abroad. Most recently she is co-author with Lynn Plimley of four books published by Paul Chapman/Sage Publications (2006/7). One of these books *ASDs in the Secondary School* was runner up in the TES/NASEN Book Awards for Teaching and Learning in 2006.

In 2002, Maggie was seconded to the Welsh Assembly Government (WAG) as a Development Officer for Inclusion in Wales with a specific responsibility for Autistic Spectrum Disorders (ASDs), Able and Talented and SEN Training in Wales. She still works closely with WAG on ASD matters. She joined the team at Autism Cymru as Deputy CEO in January 2005. She is still committed to training and consultancy work with a range of practitioners from health, social services, education, the criminal justice system and the emergency services.

LYNN PLIMLEY

Lynn trained to teach children with Special Educational Needs in the mid-1970s and since 1979, has worked with children with ASDs.

She has worked in generic special schools for primary aged children and residential schools for those with SLD. She also spent a year in a multi-disciplinary team to support the inclusion of children with learning difficulties in mainstream schools.

After spending three years as a Deputy Head in a large special school, she joined a local autistic society and developed their training and educational information services for three years, going on to become the first Principal of Coddington Court School for children aged 8–19 with ASDs in Herefordshire.

She has also worked indirectly with adults and young people on the autistic spectrum.

Currently, she works part-time as a Lecturer in ASDs at Birmingham University with their web-based course (www.webautism.bham.ac.uk). She also works for Autism Cymru, building up a series of 3 National forums for mainstream secondary school teachers, primary school teachers and special school teachers to share good practice and co-delivering LEA training with Maggie Bowen.

She tutors M.Ed dissertation students for the Course in ASDs (Distance Learning) and is a member of the internationally respected, Autism Centre for Education and Research (ACER), based at the University of Birmingham's School of Education.

The ACER Team has recently completed

- An ASD information website and factsheets for primary care practitioners for NES–NHS in Scotland – www.nes.scot.nhs.uk/asd/contacts/index/htm
- A review of support and services for young people with Asperger syndrome in Northern Ireland for the Northern Ireland Commissioner for Children and Young People (NICCY) – www.niccy.org

She is an Editorial Board member of both the *Good Autism Practice (GAP) Journal* and the *Educational Review Journal* and the Book Editor for the *GAP Journal.*

Lynn has built up a national profile of training in the importance of understanding the condition of autistic spectrum disorders for schools and care establishments.

Glossary

ABC – Antecedents, Behaviour, Consequences

ACCAC – Qualifications, Curriculum and Assessment Authority for Wales (now part of the Welsh Assembly Government)

ADHD – Attention Deficit Hyperactivity Disorder

Aetiology – the root cause of a condition or disease

APP – Accessibility Planning Project

AS – Asperger Syndrome

ASDAN – Award Scheme Development and Accreditation Network

ASDs – Autistic Spectrum Disorders

Autism Cymru – Wales' national charity for ASDs

BILD – British Institute of Learning Disabilities

DED – Disability Equality Duty

DES – Disability Equality Scheme

DfES – Department for Education and Skills (England)

DSM IV – Diagnostic and Statistical Manual (Edition 4)

GAP – *Good Autism Practice*- a Journal published by the British Institute of Learning Disabilities (BILD)

IEP – Individualized Education Programme

ICD 10 – International Classification of Diseases

INSET – IN-Service Education and Training

IT – Information Technology

NAS – National Autistic Society

NT – neurotypical

OCD – Obsessive Compulsive Disorder

Ofsted – Office for Standards in Education

PAPA – Parents and Professionals for Autism/Autism Northern Ireland (the national charity for ASDs in Northern Ireland)

PECS – Picture Exchange Communication System

Proprioception – the awareness of one's body position, location and orientation in space

Proxemics – the ability to gauge appropriate physical-social distances

PSHE – Personal Social and Health Education

SALT – Speech and Language Therapist

School Forums – developed by Autism Cymru to give teachers working with ASDs in Primary, Secondary and Special schools across Wales the opportunity to meet and exchange information

SEN – Special Educational Needs

SENDA – The Special Educational Needs and Disability Act (2001)

SLD – Severe Learning Disabilities

Social Stories – a strategy developed by Carol Gray to teach individuals with ASDs appropriate social skills

STAR – Setting, Trigger, Action, Response

SULP – Social Use of Language Programme

Vestibular – the sense of a centre of gravity and equilibrium

TEACCH – Treatment and Education of Autistic and related Communication-handicapped CHildren

Triad of Impairments – difficulties encountered by individuals with ASDs in social understanding, social communication and rigidity of thought as noted by Lorna Wing

WAG – Welsh Assembly Government

How to Use This Book

PowerPoint presentation and handouts

The enclosed CD-ROM contains a PowerPoint presentation with notes for Sections 1 to 12. We would recommend that presenters make a printout of the slides and the accompanying notes and read them thoroughly prior to use. Using the CD-ROM, participants can be given copies of PowerPoint slides at the beginning or the end of the training session. It is often useful to print out the slides as handouts with a space for note taking when they are given out for information at the beginning of a session. Although the notes are primarily intended as information and a guide for presenters, yet they can also be printed out for participants if the presenter feels this would be useful.

Details of how to access the materials using the CD-ROM PowerPoint instructions for CD-ROM

Slideshow

- To access the PowerPoint screens for this Section, insert the CD-ROM into your disk drive.
- Left double click on the file named 'My Computer' and then click on the 'Autism Inclusion Toolkit' CD Drive.
- Left double click on Section 1 and then click on the 'View' icon on your toolbar.
- To make the slides work as a continuous slideshow, click on 'Slideshow'.

Speaker Notes

- If you wish to access the Speaker notes for this Section, click on 'View' and then choose 'Notes page'.
- You may also want to print off each slide with accompanying notes. Return to 'View' and click on 'Normal'.
- Click on 'File' and then click on 'Print'. In the section 'Print what' – approximately two-thirds of the way down the box on the left, choose 'Notes Page'. You may want to adjust which Notes pages you print off by specifying their number in the 'Slides' section, immediately above the 'Print what' section. Press 'OK'.
- Adjustments can also be made to reproduce colour or black and white printing.

Handouts

To reproduce handouts for your audience from this presentation, click on 'Handouts' in the 'Print what' option. Choose how many screens you want per page in the adjacent numbered box. Press 'OK'.

Using the extension activities and case studies

Each section contains some suggested activities and some sections offer case studies for discussion. Trainers can be selective in their use of these but it is advisable to break the session up with workshop activities or time for reflection and discussion.

Recommended reading and resources

Each section contains a list of Recommended Reading and Resources. It is important to provide participants with a list of recommended reading and resources as part of the training package. This will encourage them to explore issues raised further in the training. If the school has a resource bank of some of the recommended material this will help to encourage participants to explore issues further.

Preface

A growing number of individuals with Autistic Spectrum Disorders (ASDs) are now educated in mainstream settings. The difficulties they have in relation to communication, social interaction and flexibility of thought can create problems for them in a school environment where sometimes their needs are not fully understood. A strong reaction to sensory stimulation can also make school a very stressful place. It is essential therefore that all school staff are aware of these needs in order to alleviate stress and maximize learning potential. Throughout the book we will use the term ASDs rather than Autism or Asperger Syndrome focusing on the difficulties individuals have relating to the autistic spectrum rather than a specific label.

Autism Cymru has been working successfully across Wales, facilitating 'The Inclusive Schools and ASDs : Whole School Training and Research Project' and, as a result, is aware of the need to produce high quality training materials to help all school staff to recognize the needs of individuals with ASDs. Although a number of practical texts now exist on the subject, including our own ASD Support Kit, yet we would argue that schools would benefit from a complete training package that could be delivered during staff meetings and on INSET days.

The book is divided into sections rather than conventional chapters as this seemed more appropriate for a training manual. Section 1 gives details of how the sections might be used either as a stand alone training session on a particular issue or in combination with other sections to deliver a full day or half a day of training. This Toolkit is therefore designed to meet a variety of training needs and consists of PowerPoint slides (available on the CD-ROM) with explanatory notes on the issues included within them. It also offers guidance on how best to deliver INSET in schools, providing examples of activities/case studies that can be used to facilitate discussion at the end of each topic. Recommended reading lists and resources are also included. Section 12 of this resource gives advice on how best to carry out an audit of school provision in order to inform School Development Plans, School Access and Inclusion Plans and meet the Disability Equality Duty. The last section of the book provides readers with a list of useful contacts.

1

Planning INSET and Using the Training Materials in your Setting

> This section will examine different ways of delivering INSET to colleagues, giving details of the issues for consideration, such as where should the INSET take place? What media should I use? What is the message I want to convey? Is there going to be a follow-up session? It will also suggest different ways in which schools can build up a resource bank of materials on Autistic Spectrum Disorders (ASDs). It will tell the reader about the ways in which the training package can be used in school. Some schools may want to focus on one or two particular sections, e.g. 2 and 3 to raise general awareness of ASD in the school, others may wish to focus on an issue that is causing concern, e.g. challenging behaviour. This section also offers examples of how the package can be used in a flexible way to meet individual needs.

Learning outcomes

This Toolkit can be used to deliver INSET at a number of levels. It may be important in some schools just to concentrate on raising awareness of ASDs, using Section 2, whilst in other schools that have a number of pupils with ASDs, it might be considered essential to work through a number of the sections over a period of time. It is advisable therefore to think carefully about the needs of the audience before planning a training package. Training is only valuable if participants leave enthused and ready to improve their practice. Very often people attend training sessions because they have to, not because they want to. In such circumstances, training becomes a waste of time and effort for both the facilitator and the participant.

School staff are constantly bombarded with paper work so another questionnaire to complete may not go down very well. However, it is important to have some idea of what people want to know and their existing knowledge base of ASDs. A selection of short sharp points with a tick box may be the best option. Examples of questions may include:

- Would you like to know more about Autistic Spectrum Disorders?
- Do you teach any pupils with ASDs at the moment?
- If the answer is 'No', have you ever taught a pupil with ASDs?
- Do you know about the Triad of Impairments?
- Would you like to know how to help pupils with ASDs maximize their learning potential?

A short questionnaire for this purpose is included on the CD-Rom as Figure 1.1.

Having the answers to just a few questions like this can help the facilitator to plan to meet the needs of an audience. He/she will be able to judge their level of knowledge and understanding of ASDs and whether or not the potential audience is interested in the proposal for training. Making a list of the Learning Outcomes or Expected Goals on a flip chart and referring to them at the beginning and at the end of your training can help keep facilitator and participants focused.

It is important to remember that not everyone is going to be enthusiastic about ASDs and so training does need to be as motivating as possible. Using videos/DVDs often helps in this respect. Each section of the Toolkit gives ideas about useful resources that can be used to this effect.

When and where?

The length of the training will vary depending upon the needs of your audience. The facilitator may have been tasked with raising awareness during a staff meeting, and if is this case, may have to be selective in the slides that are used. For example, he/she might decide to use a few slides from each of the first three sections – Living with ASDs, the Triad and Sensory issues or alternatively, may decide to concentrate on issues addressed in Section 6 – 'Creating an ASD-friendly Environment' and Section 12 which focuses on schools' Access and Inclusion plans and the Disability Equality Duty. He/she may find it useful to supplement basic training like this with some information about ASDs, e.g. a poster on the staff noticeboard or in reception area highlighting some of the issues relating to the Triad or containing a list of what makes an ASD-friendly environment.

It is important that at the very least staff are made aware of the issues in a staff meeting or for some time in a whole school professional development day. ASD is a disability and so the school has a legal obligation to meet the needs of pupils with ASDs as best it can. If it is difficult to persuade some staff that it is important to know about ASDs, this might be a good argument.

The Toolkit can also be used to put together a training day. Some issues or sections might be essential in this situation especially if the audience has a mixed knowledge of ASDs. We would recommend that it is important to cover issues relating to the Triad, sensory anomalies, environment and curriculum. It is also important to point out that breaktimes and lunchtimes may be particularly stressful for individuals with ASDs.

Once the core content/sections have been decided upon, the audience can then be given a choice of one or two other topics, e.g. Behaviour Management (Section 7), Tried and Tested Strategies (Section 11) or Working with Parents and other Professionals (Section 9). In order to break the day, and if two or more trainers are available, the audience could be given a choice and split into groups. This would give participants the opportunity to move around at the end of the day thus improving their concentration span and would allow them to focus on a topic that is of relevance/interest to them.

In the case of a staff meeting or a slot in the whole school professional development day, it may not be possible for the facilitator to influence where the training will take place. However, this is an issue that needs careful consideration for a whole day's INSET. The budget may be such that the training does have to take place at school and the audience may be happy with this. However, the venue still needs to be as comfortable as possible and times set aside at approximately 90-minute intervals for comfort breaks and refreshments. Seating can often be an issue. There is a need to consider how seating will be arranged based on numbers in the audience, e.g in rows (theatre style) or in groups around tables (cabaret style). If it is likely that the audience will be seated at a distance from the trainer, it may be necessary to use microphones or at least check for audibility at the start. Always make sure that any audiovisual equipment is working and can be seen and heard by the audience. However, in this respect always expect the unexpected and have contingency plans in place if a DVD/video player suddenly breaks down.

Plastic chairs can get quite uncomfortable after a long period so it is important that trainers are sensitive to this fact and watch out for times when participants are at their most fidgety. It may be that participants need a five-minute break to stretch their legs or stand up for a few moments. Some exercises suggested by the trainer in a humorous way, e.g. 'Everyone stand up. Shake your left leg! Now, shake your right leg!' can provide a bit of light relief and make people feel relaxed and ready to concentrate again.

At the end of any session, whatever the time span, provide participants with an evaluation form. Include on the form a question relating to future training needs on ASDs. Evaluation forms can be a bit daunting for the trainer/facilitator to read, especially if some participants have been negative about the presentation. It is important to view them objectively and not take any criticism too much to heart but bear any constructive comments in mind for the future. It is not unusual for some participants to comment more on the venue and the refreshments than the course content and skills of the trainer!

Building a resource bank of materials

To supplement training, it is important to build up a resource bank of materials in school. Resources might be housed in a large storage box in the library or in the staffroom. There could be a dedicated bookshelf or section in a filing cabinet with information about ASDs. Voluntary sector groups will often provide some useful information booklets and many useful articles can also be found on the Internet via the websites listed throughout this book. A number of texts and DVDs have been listed in Section 2 that can help raise awareness in a less formal way. The staff also need to be made aware that the resource bank exists via staff bulletins or the staff noticeboard.

Hints and tips for raising awareness in addition to formal training

- Information booklets for all school staff, containing basic overview of the impact of the Triad of Impairments and Sensory Issues on everyday life and what staff can do to help.
- Using moveable displays or posters in strategic places throughout the school, e.g. a large visual display or poster with a picture of child in the centre and highlighting difficulties he/she might have and how they can be overcome on either side.
- A film night to watch 'Snow Cake' or 'Rain Man' or any other dramas or films about ASDs.
- Circulating texts, such as Mark Haddon's *The Curious Incident of the Dog in the Night Time* (Vintage/UK) or Kathy Hoopmann's *The Blue Bottle Mystery* (Jessica Kingsley Publishers).
- Circulating a list of quotations from individuals with ASDs or putting them up on the staff noticeboard.
- Asking pupils with ASD to state what helps and does not help in school and circulating the information as a newsletter. It might be a good idea to include some quotations from some individuals with ASDs outside of the school to justify the points of view given (See Section 2 for examples). Do highlight pertinent issues, such as bullying and getting over-stressed.
- Using a true-or-false quiz on ASDs at lunchtime (See Figure 1.2 on the CD-Rom).
- Posters that state what makes an ASD-friendly school or conversely what does not! Sometimes people absorb what they should not do quicker than what they should do. (See Figure 1.3 on the CD-Rom.)

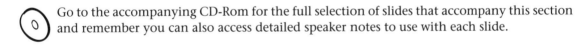 Go to the accompanying CD-Rom for the full selection of slides that accompany this section and remember you can also access detailed speaker notes to use with each slide.

Figure 1.1 Planning INSET: Questionnaire for Participants Prior to Training

Do you have any knowledge and understanding of individuals with an Autistic Spectrum Disorder? Yes/No

If yes, please give a brief explanation

....

....

....

....

....

Do you teach any pupils with an ASD? Yes/No
If yes, please give details

....

....

....

....

....

If no, have you ever taught a pupil with ASDs? Yes/No
If yes, please give details

....

....

....

....

Do you understand what is meant by the Triad of Impairment? Yes/No

Would you like to know more about ASDs? Yes/No

If yes, what topics would you like your training session to include? Please tick as appropriate:

The Triad of Impairment
Sensory Issues
Educational Implications of the Triad of Impairment
Environmental Issues
Transition
Pupil Participation
Access and Inclusion and Disability Equality Duty
Behaviour Management
Strategies and Interventions
Working with Parents

Thank you for completing this questionnaire.

Figure 1.2 True or False Quiz

TRUE OR FALSE?

1. There is no currently known cure.

2. There are more boys than girls affected.

3. The ratio of boys to girls in Asperger syndrome is 20 :1.

4. Pupils with ASD do not benefit from inclusion.

5. ASD is most prevalent amongst the middle classes.

6. ASD has close links with epilepsy.

7. ASD has only been written about in the last twenty years.

8. Families of a person with an ASD have to pay a lot of money for help.

9. People with ASD function best in a specialist environment.

10. Families often spend a lot of time finding out more about ASD.

11. Over 75% of people with ASD have additional learning difficulties.

12. People with ASD often have unusual responses to sensory stimuli.

13. There can often be another member of the wider family who is somewhere on the spectrum.

14. ASD is caused by spending too much time in front of the TV.

15. Sometimes specific drugs can help the condition.

16. Everyone with ASD has a talent in art or music or drawing.

17. Most people with ASD have an excellent memory for something that interests them.

18. People on the spectrum exist in all walks of life.

19. I will not need to alter the way I work/teach for the child with an ASD.

20. Individuals with ASD can often like routine and structure in their daily lives.

Figure 1.2 *Continued*

ANSWERS

1. **True.** ASD is a lifelong disability.

2. **True.** For Classical (Kanner's) Autism around four boys to one girl.

3. **False.** The ratio is higher in Asperger Syndrome but more like eight or nine boys to one girl.

4. **False.** By careful assessment of individual need and targeted support individuals with ASD can function well in a mainstream environment.

5. **False.** The original research carried out by Kanner and Asperger drew this conclusion because the range of individuals they studied. ASD cuts across all races, classes and ethnic groups.

6. **True.** By puberty, around a third of people with ASD have some form of epileptic activity.

7. **False.** But there has been an explosion of literature and speakers with ASD appearing at conferences over the last twenty years. For a historical look at ASD read Frith (1989) or Waltz (2005).

8. **False.** This is the impression people can get from fund-raising stories in the media.

9. **False.** Some people with ASD do live and work in specialist settings. However, each person with an ASD is unique and will have their own individual needs.

10. **True.** Many families use the Internet and support services to find out as much as they can about ASD.

11. **True.** Additional learning difficulties can occur because of the way in which they best learn.

12. **True.** Many people with ASD write and talk about their unusual responses to sensory stimuli.

13. **True.** Research in genetics has confirmed a link between ASD and the wider family.

14. **False.** There is no proven link.

15. **True/False.** There are no specific drugs for ASD but like everyone else individuals with ASD may need drugs for other medical problems.

16. **False.** This is another impression given by the media's coverage of people like Stephen Wiltshire and in films like 'The Rain Man'.

17. **True.** They have an outstanding capacity to retain information on a 'special interest'.

18. **True.** The characteristics of ASD can exist in all of us to a greater or lesser extent. Some people with ASD have very successful careers.

19. **False.** Even minor adaptation in the way that you work will benefit someone with ASD.

20. **True.** Structure and routine represent security and predictability to a person with ASD.

Figure 1.3 How 'ASD-Friendly' are you?

How 'ASD-Friendly' are you?

If you agree with the statement put a tick at the end.

- Do you think that pupils with ASD are naughty and awkward and need to mind their manners?

- Do you enjoy using sarcasm with your pupils?

- Do you insist upon blanket conformity, regardless of need and ability?

- Do you ignore the noise levels in school?

- Do you shout at pupils that you think are misbehaving or appear to be ignoring your whole class instructions?

- Do you make pupils sit and wait a long time for instruction and activity?

- Do you think that pupils with ASD are the responsibility of support staff?

- Do you think that differentiation is a waste of time and if pupils cannot understand they need to go to a special class?

- Do you always give oral instructions? After all, pupils should be paying attention?

- Do you think that it is a waste of time analysing behaviour for its communicative function?

- Do you think that parents are better kept at arm's length and should not contribute to planning?

- Do you think that parents are responsible for their children's problems?

- Do you think pupils with ASD who say they are stressed out and need some time to themselves are trying to avoid work?

- Do you punish pupils with ASD who do not bring their homework to class on time?

IF YOU HAVE ANSWERED 'YES' TO ANY OF THESE
QUESTIONS– YOU ARE NOT ASD-FRIENDLY!
DO TRY AND CONSIDER THE ISSUES THE QUESTIONS RAISE

**REMEMBER SCHOOL CAN BE A VERY STRESSFUL PLACE
FOR PUPILS WITH ASD**

The Autism Inclusion Toolkit, SAGE, 2008 © Maggie Bowen and Lynn Plimley

Section 1: PLANNING INSET AND USING THE TRAINING MATERIALS IN YOUR SETTING

1

Running INSET for Colleagues and Pupils

Key Points

- Consider your audience
- Remember about concentration spans
- Keep it light and positive
- Encourage personal reflection
- Provoke discussion
- Value feedback

2

Points for Consideration

- Is it of relevance to the participants ?
- Does it show them respect ?
- Is it objective, factual and informative?
- Is it succinct and explanatory?
- Is it delivered in an accessible way ?
- Does it give consideration to different perspectives ?
- Does it impart information that is worthwhile?
- Is it realistic?
- Does it encourage reflective practice?
- Does it act as a catalyst for improvement ?
- Do not expect things to change overnight

3

Other Considerations

- The use of an adult/child with ASDs is a powerful tool
- The use of an outside speaker can help dissolve some of the boundaries
- Video/Audio always helps
- Find out what your audience know and want to know
- Use a drip, drip message
- Maximize your approachability
- Be creative in your follow up, e.g. a focus group/visits/further reading/resource–finding

4

Responding to your Audience

- Is the location comfortable?
- Is the session going to be informal, e.g. lunch time discussion or formal, e.g. staff meeting or whole school INSET day?
- How will the seating be arranged, theatre style or cabaret?
- Will group discussion be easy to arrange?
- Will there be any refreshments?
- Where will you have a comfort break?
- How long will you wait for late comers?

5

Responding to the Audience

- Are you preparing/giving out any handouts?
- If so, will this happen at the beginning or at the end of the session?
- Do you need to provide any background information prior to the session?
- Find respectful ways to agree or disagree with any questions

6

Taking Care of Yourself

- Prepare well in advance and think about any resources you will need to hand
- Get to the venue early and test any equipment
- Prepare an opening and closing remark and point out any house/health and safety regulations
- Think about the volume and pace of your voice. If you rush too much you can make an audience feel tense

7

Take Care of Yourself

- Have a cold drink to hand
- Do not be afraid if a question is difficult; admit that you do not know the answer
- Thank everyone for coming to the INSET at the end
- Evaluation forms can help your confidence and assist in future work
- Will you be arranging a follow-up session?
- Things can go wrong, so always have a contingency plan if equipment does not work

8

Summing–up

- Think about your presentation in relation to the audience

- Know exactly what you want to achieve and how you will evaluate your success

- Remember that comfortable surroundings and refreshments are always appreciated

2

Living with Autistic Spectrum Disorders (ASDs): Same World; Different Perspectives

> ☀ We are learning more and more about the autistic spectrum from writers and speakers with ASDs. This section will begin with some basic facts about ASD and then give an overview of the thoughts of individuals with ASDs on life in general. It also includes some of their thoughts on school life in particular. It will draw on the experiences on individuals, such as Temple Grandin, Clare Sainsbury, Nita Jackson, Luke Jackson and Wendy Lawson. A range of quotations will be used to illustrate the many difficulties individuals with ASDs face in their everyday life. This section encourages both presenters and course participants to look at life from the perspective of people with an ASD.

The condition of Autistic Spectrum Disorders is one that has had an array of other names (most with the term autism mentioned somewhere) throughout its relatively short diagnostic lifespan. The conditions of autism and also of Asperger syndrome were described in the mid-1940s by two separate Austrian medical practitioners, Leo Kanner, a child psychiatrist and Hans Asperger, a paediatrician. This does not mean, however, that the condition has only existed since that time. It is possible that autism or its characteristics have existed through time, Frith (1989), Waltz (2005).

Currently, we recognize the work of both Kanner, who described a set of characteristics, also termed Kanner's autism of classic autism (Kanner, 1943) and that of Asperger who described similar characteristics and some physical differences. These two contemporaries published their research at around the same time, but by advantage of living in the USA, Kanner's work became known to the English-speaking population a long time before that of Asperger, who published in Austria in German (1944, compared to an English account of Asperger's work by Wing (1981)). A fuller historical picture can be gained from reading Wing (1996); Frith (1989); Jordan (1999).

It is difficult to know exactly how many people have an ASD as it is not always easy to identify. Some people may have an ASD and go through life without additional services, whilst others, like Wendy Lawson, may have a diagnosis in adulthood. Research undertaken by Latiff (2006) in the South Wales Valleys over a fifteen-year period suggests that is a prevalence rate of 60 per 10,000 of population. We also know that it affects more boys than girls especially at the Asperger's end of the spectrum. Professor Baron-Cohen (2003) has carried out a great deal of research into the difference between the male and female brains and argues that perhaps ASD is an extreme form of the male brain.

Often ASD does not stand alone but is associated with other difficulties, such as dyspraxia, dyslexia, Attention Deficit Hyperactivity Disorder (ADHD), Obsessive Compulsive Disorder (OCD) and Epilepsy. Sometimes the co-morbid condition can be more apparent than the ASD.

Often people with ASD can have very irregular sleeping patterns and peculiar diets or eating habits.

All individuals with an ASD are affected by the 'Triad of Impairments'. They have difficulties with social interaction, communication and rigidity of thought. The impact of the Triad is discussed in detail in Section 3. Individuals with ASD also report many sensory anomalies that affect their behaviour, such as heightened sensitivity to certain sounds, tastes, smells and textures. Sensory Issues are discussed in detail in Section 4.

Nowadays, we are learning more and more from speakers and authors with an ASD (Plimley and Bowen, 2007, pp.4–8). Their words can give us a great insight into their world and the difficulties they can face. A number of quotations are used in the presentation to draw out these issues.

Materials that can offer an insight into the world of ASDs

First person websites are very useful and are listed at the end of the Section.

Many TV dramas have recently been about the life of people with an ASD. These include Channel Four's 'The Magnificent Seven' and the BBC's 'After Thomas'. Recordings of such programmes can always be used to highlight certain issues in a down-to-earth way.

In November 2006, the BBC screened a Horizon programme which was a documentary about the life of Temple Grandin. It was called 'The Woman Who Thinks Like a Cow'.

Many people refer to the film 'Rain Man' when 'autism' is mentioned. Again excerpts from this film can be used to provoke discussion.

Ros Blackburn worked closely with Sigourney Weaver in the production of the film 'Snow Cake'. The DVD of the film is now available from www.play.com and provides a valuable insight into the world of autism.

The DVD 'A is for Autism' is a cartoon made by individuals on the spectrum and focuses on their sensory experiences. It is also available from www.play.com

Fictional books, such as Mark Haddon's best selling book *The Curious Incident of the Dog in the Night Time* (2003, 2004) published in both a child-friendly and an adult version have helped to raise awareness of ASDs.

The Blue Bottle Mystery by Kathy Hoopmann (2001) tells the story of a young boy with Asperger Syndrome and his adventures once he finds a magic bottle that grants him some wishes. The first chapter is especially useful to read as part of an INSET programme because it gives a good account of the sort of misunderstandings that can arise if a teacher is unaware of the issues and difficulties. It has been used by a number of schools to set the scene for awareness training.

Some quotations to consider...

Quotations from individuals with ASDs are always useful in helping participants to consider some of the everyday difficulties they face that we often take for granted. Quotations can be used with a variety of audiences – teaching assistants, class teachers, parents, etc. to provoke discussion. The activity can be considered by individuals followed by a group discussion, or in pairs or groups with a plenary at the end to sum up the key issues arising from the debate. It may be useful at the end of the activity to ask each participant to note one thing that they have learned from this exercise.

The following quotations from Wendy Lawson (2000, 2001) and Luke Jackson (2002) have been chosen to encourage participants to tease out some of the difficulties facing an individual with ASDs. During the activity, participants should be encouraged to think of some basic ways that they might 'build bridges' to help alleviate the stress of the individual with ASDs.

Example 1 (Lawson, 2001)

> dining rooms, TV rooms the games room and the bar are all terrifying places and I will avoid them if possible. ... Lining up for meals was very uncomfortable... When I finally arrived at the meal counter I took whatever was given to me, located a table with an empty seat to sit down at and attempted to eat my meal. Again, unfortunately I needed more time to think about what I wanted to eat, so because I hadn't taken the time I often ended with a meal I didn't like or couldn't eat! (p. 174)

Issues to consider (Presenter prompts following discussion):

- The implications of the Triad of impairments in this situation, in particular social interaction.
- Environment – noise levels, lighting, structure, lots of people.
- Preparing for choice – seeing menu before a meal to consider choice.
- Acknowledging that too much choice can cause confusion.
- Allowing time for choice and not making the individual with ASDs feel rushed into giving a quick answer. They need time to process.

Example 2 (Lawson, 2000)

Maybe if the exam had been explained to me and I had been told to read the information sheet accompanying the writing paper, I might have attempted to answer the questions. It would have been very helpful if the exam had been broken down into smaller chunks of information so that I could have worked without being overwhelmed by so many words all lumped together. (p. 42)

 Issues to consider (Presenter prompts following discussion):

- Preparing students for examination procedures – even providing written guidance beforehand.
- The language of the examination – is it ambiguous in any way? Does it contain any abstract ideas?
- A separate room devoid of distractions and ASD-friendly may need to be considered.
- Presentation – plain paper, one colour, simple and clear layout.
- Making someone available to give a prompt when it is time to move to the next question.
- Making a request for extra time.
- The use of computers or a scribe if dexterity is impaired.
- Consider asking someone with a knowledge and understanding of ASDs to scrutinize the paper before the examination.
- Look for signs that candidate may be getting distressed, e.g. rocking, flapping, twiddling, etc. and consider what should be done in these circumstances. Can you allow some time out?

Example 3 (Jackson, 2002)

'Are you listening to me?' 'Look at me when I am talking to you.' AS kids how familiar are those words? Don't they just make you groan? (And that is putting it politely!). Adults seem to make a really big deal of getting people to look at them when they are talking. Apparently it is seen as rude if you don't look at least in the direction of the speaker. The world is full of so many stupid rules. I really hate this one'. (p. 70)

Issues to consider (Presenter prompts following discussion):

- Some individuals with ASD find it uncomfortable to look at someone's eyes.
- For some using two senses at the same time – looking and listening – is very difficult. If they are not looking at you, it does not always mean that they are not listening.
- Is eye contact really worth insisting upon if it causes so much stress to the individual with ASD?
- Give rules and guidance as to when looking in the direction of someone's face may be important and suggest ways to compromise, e.g. looking at the left ear or the mouth of the speaker.
- Offer practice in conversational skills – often individuals with ASDs can be unsure when it is their turn. Even knowing when to say please or thank you can cause confusion.

Extension activities

- Use DVDs and literature suggested in the resources section to prompt discussion and encourage learning following the session.
- Search the web sites and use your own quotations – especially if you think there is a particular issue, which can sometimes be contentious, e.g. eye contact, sitting on the carpet at story time, lining up, language of the classroom that needs addressing.
- Ask participants to get into groups and think about the learning environment they find themselves in for the training. Are there any distractions? What do they like or dislike about the place? Have they understood what the speaker has said to them? Do they understand what is expected of them in the workshop activities? Ask for some feedback. Then ask them to ask themselves the same questions from the point of view of the person with ASDs.
- Ask participants to think of three things that they have learned about ASDs in this session. Ask them how they plan to 'build bridges' in relation to those things.

Recommended reading

Fictional books

Fictional books about ASDs can be very useful in raising awareness. Mark Haddon's bestseller, *The Curious Incident of the Dog in the Night Time*, is about a young man called Christopher, who is good at maths and science, but never seems to get it right with human beings. When Christopher finds a dead dog on his neighbour's lawn he decides to track down the killer and write a murder mystery about it. Christopher has a special interest in Sherlock Holmes. This book is in two versions – an adult version and a child version – and provides the reader with an insight into the world of ASDs.

Books, such as *The Blue Bottle Mystery* are written for children and show individuals in a positive light whilst still highlighting the difficulties they can face as a result of misunderstandings. Chapter One of Kathy Hoopman's book has been used successfully in INSET sessions across Wales. In just a few pages, the reader is fully aware of the fact that the hero Ben understands very little of what his teacher says to him.

Haddon, M. (2003) *The Curious Incident of the Dog in the Night Time*, (Adult Version) London: Vintage UK.
Haddon, M. (2004) *The Curious Incident of the Dog in the Night Time*, (Children's Version) London: Random House Children's Books (UK).
Hoopmann, K. (2001) *The Blue Bottle Mystery*, London: Jessica Kingsley Publishers.

First Person Accounts

There are a number of books available that have been written by individuals with an ASD who live in the UK and abroad. People like Luke Jackson and Wendy Lawson (only diagnosed with an ASD in her thirties) are now well-known speakers and writers in the field. This list of books is by no means exhaustive but does give the reader a valuable insight into so many issues. Clare Sainsbury's book is especially useful as it draws on the experiences of a number of individuals with ASDs and does contain chapters with a focus on school life.

Jackson, L. (2002) *Freaks, Geeks and Asperger Sydrome*. London: Jessica Kingsley Publishers.
Jackson, N. (2002) *Standing Down Falling up, Asperger Syndrome from the Inside Out*. Bristol: Lucky Duck Publishing.
Lawson, W. (2000) *Life Behind Glass*. London: Jessica Kingsley Publishers.
Lawson, W. (2001) *Understanding and Working with the Spectrum of Autism*. London: Jessica Kingsley Publishers.
Lawson, W. (2005) *Sex, Sexuality and the Autistic Spectrum*. London: Jessica Kingsley Publishers.
Lee O'Neil, J. (1999) *Through the Eyes of Aliens. A Book About Autistic People*. London: Jessica Kingsley Publishers.
Mitchell, C. (2005) *Glass Half Empty. Glass Half Full. How Asperger's Syndrome Changed My Life*. London: Paul Chapman Publishing/ Lucky Duck Books.
Sainsbury, C. (2000) *Martian in the Playground*. Bristol: Lucky Duck Publishing.
Segar, M. (1997) *Coping: Survival Guide for People with Asperger Syndrome*. www.autismandcomputing. org.uk/marc2.htm

Williams, D. (1992) *Nobody, Nowhere.* New York: Time Books.
Williams, D. (1996) *Autism, an Inside Out Approach.* London: Jessica Kingsley Publishers.

 Go to the accompanying CD-Rom for the full selection of slides that accompany this section and remember you can also access detailed speaker notes to use with each slide.

Section 2:

LIVING WITH AUTISTIC SPECTRUM DISORDERS (ASDS): SAME WORLD; DIFFERENT PERSPECTIVES

1

What are ASDs?

Autistic Spectrum Disorders or ASDs is a term used to describe people who have a common set of characteristics related to their ability to communicate.

People with ASDs can present the disability in a number of ways and at very different degrees. ASD can affect people of any level of intellectual ability.

2

What are ASDs?

Individuals with ASD are affected by their ability to:

• Understand and use non–verbal and verbal communication
• Interpret social behaviour, which in turn affects their ability to interact with other children and adults
• Think and behave flexibly (i.e. to know how to adapt their behaviour to suit specific situations).

Such inabilities are described as 'The Triad of Impairments'.

3

What are ASDs?

Different sub–groups within the spectrum have been described:

• Asperger Syndrome
• High Functioning Autism
• Classical Autism
• Kanner's Autism

Individuals in all these sub–groups will experience difficulties related to the Triad of Impairments.

4

How Common are ASDs?

• Estimates suggest that there are 1 in 100 people with an ASD (Baird et al., 2006) and many of these having a learning disability (LD).

• About four times as many boys as girls have an ASD in the group with LD and there may be ten times as many boys as girls in the high–ability group.

Source: Baird, G., Simonoff, E., Pickles, A., et al (2006) 'Prevalence of disorders of the autistic spectrum in a population cohort of children in South Thames: The Special Needs and Autism Project (SNAP)', *Lancet*. 368: 210-215.

5

Co-Morbidity Issues

• Some individuals with ASDs will have additional needs such as dyspraxia, dyslexia, Attention Deficit Hyperactivity Disorder (ADHD) or Obsessive Compulsive Disorder (OCD).

• They may also have difficulties with their sleeping and eating patterns.

6

Learning from Individuals with ASDs

We can learn a great deal listening to the words of individuals with ASDs.

Many of these individuals now publish about the condition to give us a greater insight into how they view the world.

7

Quinn in Sainsbury (2000)

'People probably assume I am stuck up and rude because of inappropriate responses... I have trouble determining which situations to say thank you in, how to say it and or reacting fast enough.'

Source: Sainsbury, C. (2000) *Martian in the Playground*, London: Lucky Duck/Paul Chapman Publishing.

8

Luke Jackson (2002)

'I am always being told off for standing too close to people and following them around all the time but it is difficult to know when it is right to follow someone around and carry on talking and when the conversation has ended and I am to leave them alone.'

Source: Jackson, L. (2002) *Freaks, Geeks and Asperger Syndrome*, London: Jessica Kingsley Publishers.

9

Jasmine Lee O'Neil (1999)

'Autistics can be devastated and not cry. They can react wildly to events others treat as trivial.'

Source: Lee O'Neil, J. (1999) *Through the Eyes of Aliens. A Book About Autistic People*, London: Jessica Kingsley Publishers.

10

Karen in Sainsbury (2000)

'Having fashion sense, keeping up with hygiene and socialising in larger groups of people were skills that only began to solidify for me in my years after graduating from high school.'

Source: Sainsbury, C. (2000) *Martian in the Playground*, London: Lucky Duck/Paul Chapman Publishing.

11

Sainsbury (2000)

'Many people with AS compare themselves to extraterrestrials – one woman brilliantly describes autism as "Oops wrong planet syndrome". Some find a kindred spirit in Mr Spock, perpetually baffled by the illogical behaviour of others.'

Source: Sainsbury, C. (2000) *Martian in the Playground*, London: Lucky Duck/Paul Chapman Publishing.

12

Nita Jackson (2002)

'I was sensitive to change. I was terrified of it because change leapt into the unknown and I could not get my head around the concept of what the unknown was.'

Source: Jackson, N. (2002) *Standing Down Falling Up, Asperger Syndrome from the Inside Out*, Bristol: Lucky Duck Publishing.

13

Sainsbury (2000)

'I was bullied a lot because of being odd or different and they knew they could do it to me without me fighting back or reporting it to a member of staff.'

Source: Sainsbury, C. (2000) *Martian in the Playground*, London: Lucky Duck/Paul Chapman Publishing.

14

Sarah in Sainsbury (2000)

'I began to spend more and more time in the library which I regarded as a sanctuary. I would read from various picture books…science books and journals such as Science News.'

Source: Sainsbury, C. (2000) *Martian in the Playground*, London: Lucky Duck/Paul Chapman Publishing.

15

Jack in Sainsbury (2000)

'They would not let me play with the coloured wood blocks because those were for primary kids. But I was greatly attracted to the bright colours. Maybe if they had tried to teach me using bright coloured manipulatives, even though I was older than the age they thought should be playing with them, I might have learned a little more about maths.'

Source: Sainsbury, C. (2000) *Martian in the Playground*, London: Lucky Duck/Paul Chapman Publishing.

16

Luke Jackson (2002)

'Ben has massive problems with his senses. Everything seems to be extreme with him. He spends so much time with his fingers in his ears …. He also hates wearing clothes and if he does, he has to have the labels cut out.'

Source: Jackson, L. (2002) *Freaks, Geeks and Asperger Syndrome*, London: Jessica Kingsley Publishers.

17

Wendy Lawson (2001)

'I have a need for order, therefore I constantly feel compelled to arrange and order my clothes, furniture, tableware and so on. If "things" are not in their right place I may find it difficult to know what to do next, move into the next part of a conversation, work out the next part or aspect of a procedure and so on.'

Source: Lawson, W. (2001) *Understanding and Working with the Spectrum of Autism*, London: Jessica Kingsley Publishers.

18

Wendy Lawson (2001)

'Do not take misbehaviour personally. The high functioning person with autism is not manipulative. They are seldom if ever capable of being manipulative. Usually misbehaviour is the result of efforts to survive experiences which may be confusing, disorientating or frightening.'

Source: Lawson, W. (2001) *Understanding and Working with the Spectrum of Autism*, London: Jessica Kingsley Publishers.

19

Temple Grandin (1999)

'I find great value and meaning in my life and have no wish to be cured of being myself. If you want to help me then don't try to change me to fit into your world. Grant me the dignity of meeting me on my own terms, recognize that we are equally alien to each other… . Work with me to build more bridges between us.'

Source: Grandin, T. (1999) *Genius may be an Abnormality: Educating Students with Asperger Syndrome and High Functioning Autism*, Paper presented during Autism 99 (Conference on the internet) www.autism99

20

The Impact of the Triad of Impairments on Everyday Life

> ☼ This section will explore issues around the Triad of Impairments (difficulties in communication and interaction and rigidity of thought) and how these impact on everyday life. Things we often take for granted, such as non verbal clues and body gestures are often lost on individuals with ASD. The language of schools is full of idioms and sarcasm and phrases which can easily by misinterpreted by individuals with ASDs who tend to take things literally. Their rigidity of thought and love of rules and routines can be viewed very positively at times but only if the rules and routines do not change. This section will provide strategies on how some of these difficulties might be overcome.

Rationale

The Triad of Impairments

The current terminology is autistic (or autism) spectrum disorder/s (Wing, 1996).

To have a basic understanding of the condition, it is important to know about the Triad of Impairments (Wing, 1988) – the three main areas of development where people on the autistic spectrum manifest differences.

They will all have difficulties with:

- Social Interaction
- Communication and
- Imagination/Rigidity and Flexibility of Thought

The impact of the Triad of Impairments on everyday life

Difficulties in social interaction

The first person quotations in Section 2 show that it can be difficult to join groups and make friends. Sometimes this leads to feelings of isolation and even depression. Strategies of how to make and maintain friendships may need to be learned especially as, on the surface, some individuals (like Quinn, 2000) can be considered insensitive or egocentric. Although we say 'Honesty is the best policy', yet we know that sometimes we need to tell 'little white lies' to keep our friends and family happy. For example, if we think a girl friend looks as if she has put on weight, we will avoid telling her at any cost! Individuals with ASD can be very honest; they like to tell it as it is and can often cause offence without being aware. They can also find it very difficult to understand how to react to other peoples' feelings and can respond in an inappropriate way in a sensitive situation, e.g. a funeral. Sometime their inappropriate behaviour in a public place can get them into serious trouble (see Section 6).

Difficulties in communication

As we form relationships with families, friends and others, there are a number of things we take for granted. We learn to detect mood and appreciate that using a particular tone of voice has an implied meaning. For individuals with ASD this can be a complicated process. Luke Jackson (2002) says how difficult it can sometimes be to understand what is required when an emphasis on just one word in a sentence can alter its meaning quite dramatically. Here is his example:

> **I** can't do that … implies I can't but maybe someone else can.
> I **can't** do that … implies it is not possible.
> I can't do **that** … implies I can't do that, but may be able to do something else.

Our mood is often reflected in our body language, for example, arms folded, head down can show that we are unhappy even if the words we speak state that we are not. We know when people are getting bored with our conversation because their body language can show us this. If we are bored listening to someone with ASD talking about a topic of particular interest, loss of eye contact, huffing, puffing and moving away will not end the conversation!

Idioms are used regularly by us in everyday language, e.g. 'That is the last straw!' or 'Keep your nose to the grindstone'. Phrases such as these can be confusing to individuals with ASD who take things very literally. The language of the classroom can also cause confusion. Consider just a few of the phrases we hear in school:

- 'Red table go to the Hall'.
- 'Paint the child sitting next to you'.
- 'Go and wash your hands in the toilet'.
- 'Look at the board and I will go through it with you'.

The social demands of others can often cause anxiety. It is common for us to make polite conversation about the weather, but for some individuals with ASD this would be a pointless exercise. They would have to put a great deal of effort into an activity which they considered to be of no value. We can see what the weather is like, so why speak about it ?!

Any conversation with an individual with ASD will need to be specific and unambiguous. We often use polite language implying that there is a choice when actually there is not, e.g. saying 'Shall we go to assembly?' implies a choice when really we are saying, 'We will go to assembly now'. If using instructions, it is important to name the individual even if the instruction is aimed at a group. Jackson (2002) says that maybe it is a good idea to have practice times to show the person with ASD exaggerated signs of when it is OK to talk and when it is time to listen.

Rigidity of thought

Special interests

Many individuals with ASD have a 'special interest'. This can involve the love of a sport, such as ice skating, trampolining or judo, an interest in a particular topic, such as trains or a hobby, such as stamp collecting. Often the 'special interest' can be all absorbing for the individual with ASD. This might be fine when they are in the company of people with the same interest or on their own, but can cause social difficulties when they are with people who do not share their interest. Children in particular will lose patience and friendships will not be maintained. 'Special interests' are of great value and importance to individuals with ASD; they can help relieve them of the stresses and strains of everyday life but must be used in a positive and flexible way in order to do this.

Insistence on rules and routines

People with ASD like structure in their lives and respond very well to rules and routines. They find it very difficult to cope with sudden changes in their daily routine. Nita Jackson explains:

> I was sensitive to change. I was terrified of it, because change leapt into the unknown and I could not get my head around the concept of exactly what the unknown was. I was so sensitive to the ever changing world around me, and everything I did at school was dictated by others, so I had no control. To compensate I had to exert my control by building a definite routine out of school life. (2002, p. 52)

Transfer of skills

Skills learnt in one situation are not automatically transferred/generalized to another similar situation. For example, if a person with ASD is taught to wash up at school, he/she will not easily be able to transfer these skills to the home. Something as simple as a different colour/shape of bowl or a different brand of washing-up liquid in each place could cause confusion. This transfer of skills can also apply to social interaction as Darius (Sainsbury, 2000) explains:

> I only recognize people if I see them in the same context and they wear the same clothes. It takes many years before I learn to recognize people in more than one situation or with different clothes. Even then meeting them in an unexpected situation/place will result in blank stares from me because I don't recognize them. (p. 82)

Useful resources

The resources suggested in Section 2 will be equally as important to this Section.

In addition, presenters may wish to use The ASD Teacher's Toolkit (PAPA, 2002) discussed in Section 5. This free interactive CD-Rom has a section devoted to the Triad of Impairments.

For enabling discussion about teaching emotions see:

Baron-Cohen, S. (2003) *Mind Reading: The Interactive Guide to Emotion.* London: Jessica Kingsley Publications.
Maines, B. (2005) *Reading Faces and Learning about Human Emotions.* London: Sage Publications.

Quotations

Consider the following quotations from individuals on the Spectrum. What areas of difficulty (in relation to the Triad of Impairments) do they highlight? What strategies might be used to help?

Example 1

> Asperger's Syndrome subdues my ability to think straight and rationally, to keep calm and collected even in the most trivial of circumstances. I'm not trying to blame what could be a character flaw on my condition, but that a significant number of my Asperger friends claim to experience a similar reduced capacity for calm and rational though in the face of adversity.
> Nita Jackson (2002, 66)

Example 2

> Wishing to join a conversation or group activity…(people with Asperger's) will be completely unaware of the subtle ways of initiating contact 'appropriately,' and will instead either blunder in an interrupting way, or hover around on the fringes of the group without awareness that there presence is seen as either ridiculous or creepy or even threatening.
> Joseph in Sainsbury (2000, 83)

Example 3

Luke Jackson talking about his little brother Ben:

> He also has a yellow circle dummy – it can not be oval, it can not be red; no, it has to be a circle and yellow. Boy does he scream and shout if we can't find a circle yellow dummy! The number of times we have all been running around in the evening, trying to find one whilst Ben throws a wobbly' (Jackson, 2002, 58).

 Extension activities

- Use the DVDs and literature suggested in the Resources for Section 2 to prompt discussion and encourage learning after the session.
- Consider a pupil with ASD who is known to you. Take each area of the Triad in turn and state what you consider to be the major issues. What strategies are you using to help overcome these difficulties?
- Think about a special interest a pupil you know has. How do you manage/time-limit it? Is it age-appropriate? Is it potentially hazardous? What aspects of it can you use to maximize learning potential?
- Discuss ways in which social skills can be taught in the context of the wider curriculum.
- How might you ensure that the peer group have a better understanding of ASDs?

Recommended reading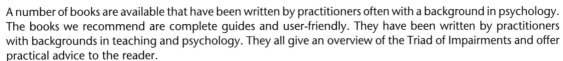

A number of books are available that have been written by practitioners often with a background in psychology. The books we recommend are complete guides and user-friendly. They have been written by practitioners with backgrounds in teaching and psychology. They all give an overview of the Triad of Impairments and offer practical advice to the reader.

Please also refer to the list in Section 2 for books written by authors with ASDs.

Attwood, T. (1998) *Asperger's Syndrome: A Guide for Parents and Professionals.* London: John Wiley and Sons. This book is a well-known text for teachers and parents across the globe. The information in the book is also useful for those labelled as having high functioning autism. The book contains detailed discussions of the problems individuals face and offers practical suggestions to help overcome or compensate for them.

Howlin, P. (1998) *Children with Autism and Asperger Syndrome: A Guide for Practitioners and Carers.* London: John Wiley and sons. This practical guide gives an overview of research, causes and 'treatment' of this complex condition. Practical approaches to language impairments, social deficits and ritualistic behaviour are discussed.

Jordan, R.R. (1999) *Autistic Spectrum Disorders – An Introductory Handbook for Practitioners.* London: David Fulton. Professor Rita Jordan is a well-known writer in the field of autism. This is a readable text that offers practical suggestions.

Plimley, L.A. and Bowen, M. (2006) A*utistic Spectrum Disorders in the Secondary School.* London: Paul Chapman/ Sage Publications.

Plimley, L.A. and Bowen, M. (2007) *Autistic Spectrum Disorders in the Early Years.* London: Paul Chapman/ Sage Publications.

Plimley, L.A. and Bowen, M. (2007) *Social Skills and Autistic Spectrum Disorders.* London: Paul Chapman/Sage Publications. The four books above form part of the series 'The ASD Support Kit'. A number of relevant issues are discussed and chapters are short and informative. Each contains a 'Reflective Oasis', which provides the reader with the opportunity to think about their current practice. The books can be read as a whole or readers can opt to dip into chapters as and when necessary.

Seach, D. (1998) *Autistic Spectrum Disorders. Positive Approaches for Teaching Children with ASD.* Stoke-on-Trent: NASEN. This book can be used by those working in mainstream or specialist settings. Diana Seach, formerly a teacher, provides information on assessment, diagnosis, alternative approaches and the curriculum. The chapter on 'supportive teaching' is particularly useful.

Wing, L. (1996) *The Autistic Spectrum.* London: Constable. Lorna Wing is best known for her research work related to the Triad of Impairment. Although over ten years old, this book provides the reader with a great insight into the minds of individuals with ASDs and offers practical guidance.

Useful websites

www.awares.org
www.autism-in-scotland.org.uk
www.autismni.org
www.nas.org
Please also refer to the websites noted in Section 2.

 Go to the accompanying CD-Rom for the full selection of slides that accompany this section and remember you can also access detailed speaker notes to use with each slide.

Section 3:

THE IMPACT OF THE TRIAD OF IMPAIRMENTS ON EVERYDAY LIFE

1

Wing's Triad of Impairments (1988)

- Impairment of social interaction
- Impairment of communication
- Impairment of imagination/rigidity of thought

Source: Wing, L. (1988). 'The continuum of autistic disorders', in E. Schoplet and G.M. Mesibov (Eds.), *Diagnosis and Assessment in Autism* (pp. 91–110). New York: Plenum.

2

Social Interaction

- socially isolated
- social demands of others cause anxiety
- finds social cues difficult to read
- may behave in a socially inappropriate way
- may lack the the strategies to establish and maintain friendships
- causing offence without being aware
- appearing egocentric or insensitive
- not knowing how to react to others' feelings

3

Communication

- may have spoken language that is formal and pedantic
- voice may lack expression
- can not understand implications of different tones of voice
- may have difficulty using and understanding non–verbal communication
- taking things literally
- inability to understand implied meaning

4

Rigidity of Thought

- Unusual and absorbing 'special interests'
- insistence on certain rules and routines
- limited ability to play and think creatively
- problems transferring skills from one setting to another

5

Strategies to help Social Interaction

- Build up awareness so that people can help to meet needs
- Use snack/lunch times to encourage turn taking and social interaction
- Reward appropriate behaviour, e.g. sharing, showing consideration
- Use games to encourage interaction, sharing and turn–taking
- Create opportunities to discuss feelings, e.g. Circle Time, PSHE lessons, music, art and drama
- Teach how behaviour affects others; soap operas can be useful
- Examine school CCTV footage
- Teach about tone of voice, facial expression and personal space– use role play, real situations
- Use Social Skills training and Social Stories
- Give a role of responsibility
- Educate the peer group

6

Strategies to help Communication

- Create the need to communicate, e.g. asking for time to explore a special interest, request for food or object, etc.
- Be explicit about expectations
- Keep language simple
- Instead of just saying 'No!', tell them what it is you want them to do
- Reward appropriate responses
- Check for understanding; do not make assumptions
- Limit choices; too many choices can cause confusion
- Teach social use of language, such as turn–taking in a conversation

7

Strategies to help Rigidity/Flexibility of Thought

- Work with family, staff and peers to ensure consistency
- Use prompt cards with pictures/texts and symbols
- Plan for change using visual timetables and social stories
- Give structure to the day using timetables and checklists
- Signal clear start and finish to activities using egg timers or a traffic light system
- Use start and finish boxes
- Organize the environment with clearly defined areas for certain activities
- Give clear visual instructions about the procedure at times of transition, e.g. PE, break, assembly, etc.
- Use special interests as a reward
- Examine special interests carefully for age appropriateness and safety
- Consider the environment and the timetable, where are problems likely to occur? Try and get the balance right between times of stress/demand and time out.

8

Three Cognitive Theories about ASDs

- Theory of Mind

- Weak Central coherence

- Executive dysfunction

9

Theory of Mind (Baron-Cohen et al. 1985)

- Difficulty in recognising that their thoughts might differ to others
- Based on a test of false belief
- Children with ASDs performed poorly compared to others of the same age, including those with Down syndrome
- Current research focuses on reading emotional states on faces

Source: Baron-Cohen, S., Leslie, A.M. and Frith, U. (1985) 'Does the autistic child have a theory of mind', *Cognition*, 21 (10): 37–46.

10

Weak Central Coherence Theory (Frith and Happe, 1994)

- Attention to detail without seeing the whole

- Inability to see 'the big picture'

- Linked to being able to read without comprehension – Hyperlexia

- Linked to being able to perform mental arithmetic and prediction (dates) at high speed

Source: Frith, U. and Happe, F. (1994) 'Autism–beyond a theory of mind', *Cognition*. 50 (1–3): 115–32.

11

Executive Dysfunction (Ozonoff, Pennington and Rogers 1991)

- Affects the ability to make a plan and work through the logical steps to achieve the goal

- Makes impulses hard to control

- Can mean that self-organization in order to settle down to work is a huge hurdle

Source: Ozonoff, S., Pennington, B.F. and Rogers, S.J. (1991) 'Executive function deficits in high functioning autistic individuals – relationship to theory of mind', *Journal of Child Psychology and Psychiatry and Allied Disciplnes*. 32 (7): 1081–122.

12

4

Sensory Issues

 This section looks at how the impact of perceiving the world in a different way through their senses has received a great contribution from many first person authors in recent years.

The writing and speaking of such people as Donna Williams (1992, 1996), Temple Grandin 1995, 1996) and Wendy Lawson (2000) has enriched our neurotypical understanding of how sensory differences and sensory distortions conspire to give a very different impression of some everyday experiences. The work of occupational therapists, such as the late Jean Ayres (1979) has enhanced our understanding of two additional sensory fields – Proprioception and Proxemics and Vestibular. This has been further developed by the work of Hinder (2004) and Bogdashina (2003). The Triad of Impairments are the key defining features of autistic spectrum disorders but it is also wise to pay attention to the additional overlay of sensory difference on functioning and behaviour as these could affect access to the curriculum; tolerance of school environments; inclusion with peers and general development.

The seven senses:

- Visual – sight
- Auditory – sound
- Tactile – touch
- Olfactory – smell
- Gustatory – taste
- Vestibular – sense of a centre of gravity
- Proprioception and Proxemics – the body's position in space and strength of physical responses

are outlined in the work of Plimley and Bowen (2006a, 2006b) as well as ideas for lessening the impact of sensory differences. Strategies that seem to help the individual with ASDs particularly are having a visual reminder (schedule or timetable) about what they are requested to do, this enables them to maintain a focus of attention; giving consideration to levels of light may be needed or the type of lighting and whether an environment is visually distracting – through having too much on display or an attractive interactive display that is hard to ignore. Sudden noise or persistent high levels of noise may interrupt the flow of concentration or make more demands upon the individual than a teacher's voice, for instance. Ways in which touch, taste and smell experiences are presented may need adjustment, again because if the sensation is overwhelming then attention will be given to trying to minimise its impact. The individual may crave more intense physical experiences where their sense of balance is challenged (vestibular) by swinging upside down or spinning round and round and this can pose health and safety concerns in any environment. The individual's concept of their body position in space (proxemics) may mean that they have little idea of how close or distant to be to others or how to orient their body towards the speaker and/or the activity. Finally, the use of physical power to push/pull/touch gently/grasp (proprioception) may be too much or too little to the requirements of the situation. Physical force may be too light (in opening a door for instance) or gripping others may be too severe (holding hands for instance) because the messages from the muscles to the individual's brain may not be transmitted correctly.

Bogdashina (2003) includes a very useful Sensory Profile that can be compiled through consultation with parents and draws together many of the differences in sensory perception that first person authors have reported. This would be a useful beginning point for staff and parents to discover precisely what the individual with ASDs is finding hard to accommodate within the school and home environment. Staff will also need to know that individuals with sensory differences may have an acute (hyper) sensitivity or a dulled (hypo) sensitivity or a fluctuation in terms of how they experience sensations.

Many individuals with ASDs are visual learners, but not all use this as their primary sense for information. Staff will need to determine how the individual is learning from teaching experiences and tailor their delivery to suit the learning style. This is equally true in teaching an individual with a sensory impairment and it is important that the individual with ASDs is accorded the same consideration. Where the individual with ASD appears to use multi-sensory approach, learning should be presented to accommodate this. If the individual uses an unusual sense to acquire information (like smelling or tasting), then strategies will need to be in place to blend information from other sensory sources and prove its reliability, whilst working with the individual on the understanding that olfactory and gustatory exploration may not be appropriate.

Useful resources

First person websites – see later list and look at http://trainland.tripod.com/sensory.htm, where there is a wealth of information, contacts and ideas on sensory differences for parents and professionals.

'A is for autism', available from www.play.com. This short Channel Four film uses cartoons developed by individuals with ASDs to give strong messages and examples of sensory differences that people of the spectrum have reported. The use of commentary by such people as Temple Grandin highlights why the effects of sensory difference can often be overwhelming.

'Outside In' a video with adults with Asperger syndrome. This resource was made by a person with Asperger syndrome who talks of his own experiences in coping with everyday life and also interviews two college friends about how they manage their Asperger syndrome. Available from http://www.nas.org.uk/nas/jsp/polopoly.jsp?d=434&a=5093

Occupational therapy resources for working on sensory integration – ask your local occupational therapists.

How do you feel, Thomas?, Published by Egmont Books, available from www.amazon.co.uk. A set of books using Thomas the Tank Engine characters to illustrate different emotional states. Thomas is a very popular 'character' with people with ASDs and so his iconic image is used to get across information about emotions.

Walker, Jones, E. (2005) *My brother Gwern.* Available free from www.autismcymru.org . This well-illustrated dual language (English/Welsh) book contains child-friendly information about a sibling (Gwern) in the family with ASD. It deals sensitively with sensory difference as well as other features of a young child with ASD, from his sister's point of view.

 Case studies

The following case studies deal with sensory differences often manifest in ASD by giving examples across a broad age range. The types of sensory differences are typically reported by parents/teachers/staff in a range of provisions. The information is intended to give a problem-solving focus and is tailored to the reader looking at what the behaviour may represent; how a staff team may respond and what particular strategies they may choose. A list of how to further use these studies appears in the extension activities section.

Early Years – Joel aged 3
Joel is a three-year-old who dislikes the loud and sudden noises of his peers. He pushes away other children and covers his ears with his hands for any activities that involve noise. This behaviour is particularly critical during free play times.

Continued

- What strategies could be put into place to lessen the impact of this sensory sensitivity ?

Primary – Minnie aged 6

Minnie has a lot of trouble with being in a line or queue with her classmates. As most movement around the school involves an initial line-up, her protestations come to a head when lining-up to come inside from the playground.

- What strategies could be put into place to lessen the impact of this sensory sensitivity ?

Secondary – Tom aged 11

Tom cannot stand wearing his tie in school and says that it feels like he is being strangled. Different types of tie fittings have been tried but he still feels uncomfortable. This is particularly true during the Winter when wearing a tie is an expectation. Polo shirts during the summer do not cause the same problems.

- What strategies could be put into place to lessen the impact of this sensory sensitivity ?

Special – Frankie aged 16

Frankie loves to find the highest point in any environment and he sits making clapping noises to hear the sound reverberate around him. He has recently discovered an easy access to the flat roof of his special school and will make every attempt to get up on the roof. He also enjoys spinning on one heel in often inappropriate places, like the dining room. The staff are concerned about Health and Safety issues and wonder if he needs a more secure environment.

- What strategies could be put into place to lessen the impact of this sensory sensitivity ?

Residential – Emma aged 13

Emma is a very fussy eater and will also not eat food that is touching on a plate. She insists that all of her food is yellow in colour and this leads to very limited choices – cornflakes; sweetcorn; yellow peppers; swedes; butter; banana milkshakes or smoothies. Staff are worried that her strong preferences might lead to malnutrition.

- What strategies could be put into place to lessen the impact of this sensory sensitivity ?

Young adult – Lee aged 15

Lee is a growing fifteen-year-old who objects to any attempts to encourage personal hygiene. He shows a sensitivity to stronger perfumes and regularly pushes away or ignores significant people in his life (mother, father, sisters, teacher) if they are wearing cosmetics or scents that he does not like. He, however, appears not to notice that at times his own body odour is unbearable.

- What strategies could be put into place to lessen the impact of this sensory sensitivity ?

 Extension activities

- Use case studies for small group discussions – compile ideas on whiteboard or flipchart paper.
- Use group problem solving to raise particular current issues and look at school and staff expectations in terms of conformity.
- Ask an occupational therapist to run an experiential workshop to raise issues of sensory integration.

Continued

- List staff sensory likes and dislikes to raise awareness of preferences in us all.
- Hold whole staff discussion on issues of conformity, tackle the spectre of 'I cannot treat him differently' by locating that attitude within a wider disability arena
  - Look at dress code issues.
  - Assess noise levels around school.
  - Facilitate safe activities that challenge the centre of gravity.
  - Work with parents and carers to extend eating/clothing tolerances.
  - Lining-up – is it a crime to always want to be first ?
  - Consider the option to sit on a chair instead of the carpet.
  - Appropriate personal distance – will it be as charming (as it is for the 4-year-old now) for a 22-year-old to invade your personal space ?
- Look at the dissemination of information about sensory difference to the whole staff group, especially looking at the issue of conformity. Whole staff teams include administrative, building, lunchtime, care, medical and transport workers – strategies adopted by classroom or care staff need to be shared with those who could also help promote a consistent approach.

Recommended reading

Bogdashina, O. (2003) *Sensory Perceptual Issues in Autism and Asperger Syndrome Different Sensory Experiences Different Perceptual Worlds*. London: Jessica Kingsley Publications. This is a comprehensive introduction to the role of sensory differences in ASDs and contains the useful Sensory Profile checklist mentioned earlier in this section.

Chara, K.A., Chara, P.J. with Chara, C. (2004) *Sensory Smarts: A Book for Kids with ADHD or Autism Spectrum Disorders Struggling with Sensory Integration Problems*. London: Jessica Kingsley. Very well illustrated information about how sensory differences may be manifest in the individual.

Grandin, T. (1995) 'How people with autism think' in Schopler, E. and G. B. Mesibov, (eds), *Learning and Cognition in Autism*. New York: Plenum Press. First-person account of how Temple views and processes the world around her.

Grandin, T. (1996) *Thinking in Pictures and Other Reports from my Life with Autism*. California: Vintage Press. First-person information conveys a powerful message of the impact of Temple's visual processing approach to any information.

Myles, Brenda, Smith and Southwick, J. (2001) *Asperger Syndrome and Sensory Issues: Practical Solutions for Making Sense of the Real World*. Shawnee Mission, Kansas: Autism Asperger Publishing Company, 2001. Comprehensive account of sensory issues: in Asperger syndrome and a wealth of ideas and strategies to alleviate some of the common issues.

Plimley, L. A. and Bowen, M. (2006a) *Autistic Spectrum disorders in the secondary school*. London: Paul Chapman/ Sage Publications. This and the following title gives a foundation to understanding sensory difference and how to counteract some of its impact in school according to age group and, below, to staff working in support roles.

Plimley, L. A. and Bowen, M. (2006b) *Supporting Pupils with Autistic Spectrum Disorders*. London: Paul Chapman/ Sage Publications.

Williams, D. (1992) *Nobody, Nowhere*. New York: Time Books. The author was one of the first people with ASD to give a strong message about how sensory differences are experienced by individuals with ASDs. This is her first autobiographical account and her later publications look at sensory features in more depth.

Williams, D. (1996) *Autism an Inside Out Approach*. London: Jessica Kingsley Publications.

Useful websites

These are all websites run by people on the autistic spectrum. They are imaginative, creative, inspirational and give a good insight into how people on the spectrum think.

www.autastics.org
www.aspiesforfreedom.com
www.aspie.com
www.jimsinclair.org
http://ani.autistics.org

www.donnawilliams.net
http://www.geocities.com/CapitolHill/7138/laurence.htm
www.spidernet.nl/martijn_dekker/otsp/miedzianik.html
http://ani.autistics.org/jane.html

 Go to the accompanying CD-Rom for the full selection of slides that accompany this section and remember you can also access detailed speaker notes to use with each slide.

Section 4:

SENSORY ISSUES

1

Sensory Differences

- Hyposensitivity – means that awareness is not finely tuned

- Hypersensitivity – means that sensations can be experienced as acute and overwhelming

- Inconsistency of perception – levels of hypo and hypersensitivity can fluctuate or not be present at times

2

Visual Differences

- Visual distortions
- Perception can deceive – dimensions
- Use of focus
- Combination gives some differing visual perceptions of situations.
- Dyslexia and coloured Irlen lenses
- Strong likes and dislikes in terms of patterns, colours and sequences
- Visual order

3

Auditory Differences

Hearing anomalies

- Their attention can appear as if it is elsewhere.

- Responses in an under– or over–reactive way to different auditory stimuli.

- Acute awareness of noises that we do not notice.

- Fingers over their ears or partially covering the outer ear.

4

Tactile Differences

Tactile defensiveness
- Over-reaction to any type of unwanted tactile sensation
- Some people with ASD report feeling assaulted by the touch of others
- Many prefer firm holds and grasps
Intolerance – textiles and other tactile experiences
- Dislike of new clothing
- Not being able to wear certain fabrics
- Fastidious about not getting dirty

5

Taste and Smell Differences

Taste/Smell predominance

- Strong preferences likely for particular tastes and smells.

- It may be difficult to introduce new taste experiences or deviate from the 'tried and tested'.

- Taste and smell gives main information about the world – tasting anything new or smelling everything before complying with an instruction.

6

Vestibular Differences

- Sense of balance and knowing our capacities
- Craving 'risky' sensations – balancing on thin supports or climbing to the top of precarious heights
- Often love spinning, rocking, seesaws
- Seeking out experiences that challenge the centre of gravity and balance

7

Proprioceptive and Proxemic Differences

- Knowing how to keep a suitable distance from others
- May affect
  - How body is oriented in space
  - The strength of hand-grasp
  - The amount of awareness of objects, furniture and people around them
- Fixed sense of personal boundaries
- Proprioception is feedback from muscles and joints, helping maintain posture and be aware of limbs and body in space.

8

Film
'A is for autism'

(Available from www.play.com)

9

Ideas

- Build a profile of differences
- Look at critical issues in school
- Consider
  - Lenses
  - Earphones/headphones
  - Movement before or after main school
  - Work with home on introducing new experiences
  - Teach distance/ awareness of strength
  - Offer safe centre of gravity activities

10

Environmental Adaptation

- Think carefully about the experiences you are offering
- If a person objects because of sensory sensitivity, how can you adapt the situation for them?
- If that objection is loud and disruptive, what is to be gained from insisting?
- Would you make a person with another sensory disability operate in a situation if they could not function, understand or appreciate?

11

5

The Educational Implications of Autistic Spectrum Disorders (ASDs)

 This Section will look at ways in which the Triad of Impairments can impact life at school. It will make reference to situations that may cause anxiety and offer strategies to help. It will also give an overview of all the main National Curriculum subjects detailing the difficulties that may arise and suggest ways to overcome these.

Despite their differences in intellectual ability, individuals with ASD all share a common set of characteristics known as the Triad of Impairments. This means that they have difficulties with social and emotional interaction, all aspects of communication regardless of their language level and a lack of flexibility in their thinking and behaviour. We know from the writings of individuals with ASD, such as Wendy Lawson and Temple Grandin, that they also have very different responses to sensory experiences. All these difficulties will impact the way they react in the school situation. The PowerPoint slides and handout notes give the reader detailed information about school issues.

Useful resources

ACCAC (2000) *A Structure for Success: Guidance on the National Curriculum and Autistic Spectrum Disorders,* Birmingham: ACCAC. In 2000, this document was circulated to all schools in Wales and it can be downloaded from the Welsh Assembly Government website. It examines key issues such as managing learning, planning the whole curriculum, access to the National Curriculum and working in mainstream schools with pupils with ASDs. Access from http://old.accac.org.uk/eng/content.php?mID=167

Parents and Professionals Autism (PAPA), Department of Education, Department of Education and Science, NI (2003) *Autistic Spectrum Disorders – A Teacher's Toolkit. CD-Rom.* This is an excellent interactive CD-Rom covers a range of issues such as teaching strategies, curriculum issues, behaviour management and writing IEPs. There are video clips to watch and materials to print. This CD-Rom is without copyright. Visit www.autismni.org

Department for Education and Skills (2002) *Autistic Spectrum Disorders: Good Practice Guidance.* Nottingham: DfES. This document is in two parts – 01 'Guidance on Autistic Spectrum Disorders,' and 02 'Pointers to Good Practice.' Telephone: 0845 602260. www.dfes.gov.uk/sen

🗁 Case studies

Early Years – Charlie aged 4

Charlie has a special interest in lego bricks and would spend the day building towers if he is left to do so. He also enjoys watching Thomas the Tank Engine videos. Charlie's teacher has

Continued

provided him with a visual timetable consisting of picture symbols. Each day, she shows him the timetable so that he knows exactly what is going to happen. When each activity is to end a bell rings and he is allowed to tear off the symbol from the timetable. This seems to work well except at break times and lunch times when Charlie gets very aggressive with the other children.

What strategies can Charlie's teacher put in place to ensure that the whole of Charlie's day runs smoothly?

 ## Issues to consider

Break times and lunch times can lack structure. Charlie may find the change in environment and sensory experiences in the playground or the dining hall stressful. Breaktimes and lunchtimes can also be times when other children can be noisy and unpredictable. Charlie may need opportunities for some time out during these times to focus on a special interest.

 ## Case studies

Primary – Ali aged 8

Ali is eight years old. Whenever the teacher reads a story to the rest of the class as part of the English lesson, Ali looks out of the window and appears not to be listening. Often his teacher gets very angry and insists he looks in her direction and pay attention. This sometimes results in Ali becoming confrontational.

What strategies might be put in place to avoid confrontation?

 ## Issues to consider

Sometimes individuals with ASDs find it difficult to use two senses at once. Ali may need to look away from the teacher to concentrate on listening to her voice. The teacher should not assume that he is not listening because he is not looking at her. She should check for understanding and not insist upon eye contact.

Ali, like many with an ASD, is likely to be a visual learner. Story books that have illustrations might be of more interest to him. As Ali is a good reader, he could be given his own copy of the story to read to himself as the teacher reads to the class.

 ## Case studies

Secondary – Josef aged 14

Josef sometimes has problems working along side his peers in Art and Design. When groups of pupils are expected to work together to design a model or piece of equipment, Josef always stands on the edge and is reluctant to participate.

How can the teacher encourage Josef to take an active part in the lesson?

Issues to consider

Josef may need his own set of visual instructions (written or pictorial) to complete the task as it is likely that his sequencing skills are poor. He may find the concept of trying to imagine something that he can not yet see, difficult to grasp. Providing him with some pictorial examples might help increase his confidence. Josef may feel frustrated if his motor skills restrict him from making a good job of the exercise. He may be concerned that both his peer group and teacher will criticize his contribution. Every effort should be made to boost his self-esteem. Giving Josef a defined role in the group might also help, e.g. recording his group's work.

 Case studies

Young adult – Ollie aged 16

Ollie is due to leave school in September. He is keen to attend his local College of Further Education to pursue his interest in ICT. He has a broad curriculum and is following some GCSE courses and the school place transferable key skills outlined in the National Qualifications Framework. Certain key skills are also addressed within his PSHE programme and other social skills programmes. Ollie is not very independent and still relies heavily on adult support.

What issues need to be addressed in an individual leaver's programme for Ollie?

 Issues to consider

Key issues for consideration should include life skills (increasing independence), leisure skills, core skills, accreditation (including wider accreditation, such as Duke of Edinburgh and ASDAN), careers and work experience. Transition planning for the move to college will need to be planned well in advance and opportunities for familiarization visits provided.

 Extension activities

These activities can be adapted for use with practitioners from different educational backgrounds and settings. Some are intended for individual reflection whilst others would be better as small group discussion exercises. It might be useful for the trainer to use one of each kind dependent on the partcipants' needs and background.

- Ask participants to think of a child in their class and to note the difficulties he/she is having in a curriculum area. Ask them to think of three strategies that might help.
- Make up your own case study examples based on real life situations you have known.
- Devise a quiz to check that participants have understood about the impact of the Triad of Impairments on National Curriculum subjects.
- Appoint a scribe and ask participants to discuss what they consider to be good practice when planning for transition and planning for work experience. Collate the responses on a flip chart and circulate after the training.
- Life skills and sex education will need addressing. Ask participants to consider ways in which they can enable this as part of the wider curriculum.

Continued

- Highlight certain problem areas, such as inability to relate to others, lack of empathy and difficulties in generalizing learning. In small groups, ask participants to brainstorm possible solutions. Record on a flip chart, e.g. Problem: Generalizing learning. Solution: Use prompt cards with text/pictures/symbols.
- Individuals with ASDs can have problems with bullying at school. What systems are in place to combat this especially at break and lunchtimes?

Use the CD-Rom : *Autistic Spectrum Disorders – A Teacher's Toolkit* produced by Parents and Professionals Autism (PAPA) Department of Education, Department of Education and Science, NI (2003) and available from Autism Northern Ireland, Donard, Knockbracken Healthcare Park, Saintfield, Belfast, BT8 8BH; Tel: 0208 9040 1729; Email: info@autismni.org; Website: www.autismni.org

Recommended reading

The texts have been chosen because they are school-focused and discuss a range of useful strategies.

Betts, S.W., Betts, D.E. and Gerber-Eckard, L.N. (2007) *Asperger Syndrome in the Inclusive Classroom. Advice and Strategies for Teachers.* London:Jessica Kingsley. This is a commonsense, practical book full of advice and strategies. It examines such areas as curriculum, transport, unstructured time, assembly and whole school approaches.

Cumine, V. et al. (1998) *Asperger Syndrome: A Practical Guide for Teachers,* London: David Fulton. and Cumine, V. et al. (2000) *Autism in the Early Years. A Practical Guide.* London: David Fulton.

Val Cumine, and her co-authors (all with a background in education) provide sound advice, tips and strategies in an informal and highly readable way. They also encourage readers to look at things from the perspective of the individual with an ASD, especially when examining behaviour management.

Hayward, A. (2006) *Making Inclusion Happen.* London: Paul Chapman Publishing. Anne Hayward's book tackles inclusion in the broader context and is invaluable for those wanting to learn more about the Every Child Matters agenda.

Hanbury, M. (2005) *Educating Pupils with Autistic Spectrum Disorders: A Practical Guide,* London: Paul Chapman Publishing. Martin Hanbury has an extensive experience of working with youngsters with ASDs and his book contains some useful photocopiable INSET materials. It also contains some handy hints and checklists.

Pittman, M. (2007) *Helping Pupils with Autistic Spectrum Disorders to Learn.* London: Paul Chapman Publishing. This book focuses on helping children with ASDs to understand the notion of change in their daily routines so that this understanding has a positive effect on their behaviour and ability to access the curriculum.

Plimley, L.A. and Bowen, M. (2006) *Autistic Spectrum Disorders in the Secondary School.* London: Paul Chapman/ Sage Publications.

Plimley, L.A. and Bowen, M (2007) *Autistic Spectrum Disorders in the Early Years.* London: Paul Chapman/Sage Publications. The above two books are part of a series of books in The ASD Support Kit. They focus on a range of issues dependent on the educational setting. Individual chapters can be used to supplement training and the 'Reflective Oasis' help practitioners to re consider and evaluate their teaching methods.

Seach, D. (1998) *Autistic Spectrum Disorders. Positive Approaches for Teaching Children with ASD.* Stoke-on-Trent: NASEN. Diana Seach offers advice and guidance in a concise and practical way on a wide range of issues, such as access to the curriculum, writing IEPs, partnership with parents and supportive teaching strategies.

Wall, K. (2004) *Autism and Early Years Practice.* London: Paul Chapman Publishing. Kate Wall's examines the early years curriculum in detail in addition to giving a detailed overview of the possible services available.

Useful websites

www.awares.org
www.wales.gov.uk
www.dfes.gov.uk/sen
www.dfes.gov.uk/curriculum_pre-entry/
www.ipsea.org.uk
www.inclusion.org.uk
www.autism-in-scotland.org.uk
www.autismni.org

www.nas.org.uk
www.qca.org.uk/qualifications
www.asdan.org.uk

 Go to the accompanying CD-Rom for the full selection of slides that accompany this section and remember you can also access detailed speaker notes to use with each slide.

Section 5:
THE EDUCATIONAL IMPLICATIONS OF AUTISTIC SPECTRUM DISORDERS (ASDS)

1

The Educational Implications of ASDs

- Let us examine some of the common issues facing mainstream school teachers using the framework of the Triad of Impairments.

- Note the differences in social interaction, communication and flexibility of thought and behaviours.

2

Differences in Social Interaction

- Low tolerance of peer group
- Dislike of sharing or taking turns
- Play activities and/or social behaviours inappropriate
- Play skills restricted
- Shows no desire to investigate or explore
- Little or no empathy for others

3

Differences in Social Interaction continued

- Socially aloof or awkward

- Restricted interests

- Simple social actions are often a complicated process(lining up,personal space, dialogue)

4

Differences in Communication

- Understands some simple instructions
- Expresses own desires/selfishness
- Lack of motivation to communicate
- Limited understanding of the attempts of others
- Does not enjoy shared social situations
- Use of gesture, voice intonation, non-verbal expression limited and unable to understand their use by others
- Makes factual points in conversation

5

Differences in Communication continued

- Needs to think carefully before responding
- Appears not to 'hear' what has been said
- Limited conversational skills
- Talks about a topic of interest endlessly and can manipulate conversations around to this topic

6

Differences in Rigidity of Thought and Behaviour

- Finds pretend play/drama/role play difficult
- Unable to use imagination to create models or pictures - images are derived from others
- Encounters problems in social games - turn–taking, winning, a draw
- Play can be repetitive
- May imitate behaviour but not necessarily for the reason one would expect

7

Differences in Rigidity of Thought and Behaviour continued

- Difficulties judging the cause and effect of their own behaviour

- Black and white rigid views

- Sarcasm or subtle jokes (unless they are visual and obvious, e.g. Mr Bean) are misunderstood or lost

- Does not create spontaneously without a model or intensive input

8

Common Subject Difficulties within the First Three Key Stages of the National Curriculum

9

English

Fine motor skills, creativity and imagination, comprehension of written word, literal understanding, speaking and listening skills, performing in front of others and valuing the efforts of others, drafting and re–drafting

10

Maths

- Abstract pattern work - algebra, estimation, application of concepts and rules to suit other situations
- A love of precision and accuracy may prohibit them 'having a go'
- Mental arithmetic abilities may appear better than they actually are

11

Art and Technology

- Imagination, creativity, use of relevant colour, literal interpretation of instructions, lack of evaluative skills, fine motor dexterity
- Seeing the relevance of the creative activity
- Difficulties appreciating the styles/creative works of others

12

RE and History

- Poor concept of time, life without our amenities, lack of imagination, empathy, abstract nature of God and Jesus
- Difficulty understanding the impact of events upon people and upon civilizations
- Getting 'stuck' in an era as a special interest

13

PE/DANCE/DRAMA

- Fluidity of movement, imagination, gross motor co-ordination, balance, team games and rules; empathy
- Seeing things from someone else's point of view
- Dependence on another model to copy

14

Geography

- Poor concepts of space, other cultures, different ways of life, time zones and climatology.

Science

- Considering hypotheses, carrying out tests, applying concepts and transferring skills and knowledge.

15

Basic approaches

- Make daily activities into routines
- Giving meaningful and motivational rewards
- Be predictable, consistent and reliable
- Check for understanding
- Avoid abstract terms, jokes, figures of speech or sarcasm
- Encourage the wider social circle to adopt the same approaches
- Provide opportunities for the transfer of skills

16

Positive suggestions from Good Practice Guidance (DfES, 2002)

- Visual clues to the plan, content and aims of the lesson

- Written/symbol/picture prompts for the individual

- Predictable patterns for the pupil to recognize

- Regular routine instructions

- A permanent reference system for the pupil to consult and be a more independent learner

- High expectations, the pupil does not <u>need</u> to be dependent upon adult support

Source: Department for Education and Skills/Department of Health (DfES) (2002) *Autistic Spectrum Disorders: Good Practice Guidance*. Nottingham: DfES.

17

Creating an ASD-Friendly Environment

 This section looks at the current trend towards developing practices and environments to be more disability-friendly.

Educational initiatives have looked at creating dyslexia friendliness within schools in the Primary phase (Pavey, 2007) and Autism Cymru's Inclusive schools and ASDs training programme on offer to all 22 Welsh LEAs has, as its subtitle, 'ASD Friendly schools.' It would be a fallacy to believe that the validated 'friendly' school for any disability has got all of the answers or all of its features right. However, an awareness of important features which is renewed via staff training/meetings is a step in the right direction.

Before attempting to address questions of ASD-friendly environments it must be emphasized that people who live with, work with and care for individuals with ASD need to have the understanding of the condition and appreciate the way in which fundamental differences can prejudice an individual's responses to environments. As a general rule of thumb, individuals with ASD find the following situations and times during the school day problematic:

- Playground
- School assemblies
- Lunchtimes
- Movements around the school
- Locating facilities
- Holding onto their possessions
- Having the right equipment
- Communal situations (changing rooms; toilets)
- Social interactions with others
- Working with others
- Changes in timetable
- Understanding instructions.

The work of Plimley (2004) and Whitehurst (2006) has looked at ASD specific environments to try and ascertain some important factors that would help the individual with an ASD to feel less anxious and stressed. Plimley worked with a group of students who were undertaking a postgraduate course in ASDs to distil features that they (with backgrounds in health and education) felt were important to ASD-friendliness. The list that they came up with highlighted, such things as calm and orderly environments; quiet, calm atmosphere with an absence of sudden and unpredictable noises; planning for and forewarning of changes in the school day; paying attention to lighting and heating factors and enabling pupils to choose ambient features via adjustable controls. The students also came up with important 'human' attributes that individuals with an ASD appear to feel comfortable with:

- Understanding staff
- ASD knowledge

- Prioritizing the important
- Weighing up issues
- Consistency
- Continuity
- Attitudes and anticipation
- Evaluation
  Plimley (2004: 36)

Further research by Plimley (2004) with a different set of students gave a design activity to decide on a living environment for individuals (age immaterial) with students giving a rationale for choices of colour, wall and floor coverings, lighting and heating features as well as furniture choices. Both research activities yielded ideas that paid attention to sensory differences (see Section 4); looked at comfort factors and choices of seating, working, relaxing and came up with suggestions for what would be termed a 'least restrictive environment.'

Whitehurst (2006) developed some of these ideas further and her school worked in tandem with architects to create a new suite of buildings. Humphreys (2005), an ASD-aware architect, developed a series of important principles which should be incorporated design for people with ASDs:

1 Sense of calm and order
2 High level of natural light and ventilation
3 Reduction of detail
4 Good proportion
5 Proxemics
6 Good acoustics
7 Durable materials
8 Safety and security that environment offers
9 Good observation points for staff and pupils.

These were translated into:

- Choice of communal areas
- Outdoor space
- Curved surfaces
- High-level windows
- Soft, non-flickering lights
- Underfloor heating
- Sound-absorbent ceilings.

It has to be recognized that these are situations where planning and consultation played a good part in providing what were seen as optimum conditions. However, not all people who live or work with individuals with ASD have the opportunity to start from scratch. A lot of school buildings were built post-World War II or even way before that. The PowerPoint screens acknowledge that designing new environments is not in the gift of the majority and offer suggestions for principles and adaptations that could be implemented.

 Case studies

These case studies have been constructed to give problem solving examples of typical situations where a staff team may want to look at the impact of the environment upon the individual with ASDs. Select a typical issue or a particular setting or age range to raise the issue of environmental management/adaptation.

Nursery – Jonty aged 3½

Jonty, aged three-and-a-half spent a lot of his half-day in nursery, hiding under tables with his fingers in his ears. On the rare occasions when he was coaxed out into the room, he kept a distance between himself and the other children. He pushed others away when they

Continued

came too close. He was not attracted to play with the toys, except for the sand tray, where he loves to sift sand between his fingers. He would not sit at a group table, not even for drinks and fruit.

- How could Jonty be encouraged to join in more the Nursery ?

Primary – Simeon aged 7

Simeon does not like the playground. He walks around the perimeter of the space with his eyes fixed on a particular tree. Occasionally, he approaches other children and tries to join in their games, but his approach is over-the-top and the other children can get hurt when he pulls and pushes them. If children are playing noisily he tries to shout over the noise and then gets distressed.

- How could Simeon be encouraged to make appropriate approaches to others? How could he be helped to overcome his sensitivity to excessive noise ?

Secondary – Vicki aged 12

Vicki has a real problem understanding the non-verbal gestures of Mr Brown in Maths. Mr Brown, through his years of teaching, has developed a series of gestures, looks and pauses to convey specific meanings to his pupils. He uses an arm movement to indicate 'it's time to get on with written work;' he stares intently at anyone who is talking until they notice him and when he gives instructions and he notices that someone is not looking at him he will stop what he is saying until they attend. Vicki has recently been in detention because she did not notice that Mr Brown had paused and was staring at her when she was looking out of the window while she listened to him.

- How can Mr Brown modify his non-verbal gestures to make more explicit expectations for Vicki ?

Special – Jaswinder aged 15

Jaswinder never seems to have the right equipment for the school day. Although there is a home–school book with reminders in about PE kit, swimming trunks and Wellingtons for outings, he never seems to bring the right things on the right day. English is not spoken at home, but Jaswinder understands what is needed when his teacher goes through kit requirements on the day before they are needed. Jaswinder can read some words, but responds really well to pictorial representations or digital photographs.

- How can we help Jaswinder be more responsible to bring in the right equipment on right day ?

Residential – See Yung aged 9

See Yung will not share her belongings with other children. Not only does this include her own possessions but it is also any resources, toys or equipment in her residential home that she has taken a fancy to. Any attempt to help her to play with others is strongly and vociferously objected to. Currently she has hoarded several DVDs and books in her room and when staff have tried to return them to the open area, she has made a great fuss.

- How can See Yung be encouraged to share resources with others and return home resources back to their rightful place ?

Young adult – Jack aged 19

Jack has got himself a job at the local library, tidying shelves and returning books to their correct categories. His employer is impressed by his hard work and his insistence on only taking breaks and lunch for the exact prescribed times. However, his work practices seem inefficient and labour intense. He will only take five books at a time on the trolley to return

Continued

them to the shelves. Books over his limit of five are left on the counter or the floor until he returns to collect them. This gets in the way of customer and staff access and could be a potential health and safety hazard.

- How can Jack's employers work with him to teach him a more efficient system of dealing with returned books ?

 Extension activities

Use the information on screen 11 – 'Clarity' to work together in small groups on the following areas:
- Allowing time to process verbal instructions
- Breaking down larger tasks or concepts into smaller steps
- Developing more visual resources for communication
- Identifying ways in which new skills and concepts can be generalized.

Giving enough time to process

Use a linguist on the staff to illustrate what typically happens when we are met with instructions we do not understand. Ask this person to use his or her foreign language skills to deliver a fluent and rapid 2–3 part instruction, e.g. Get out your pens, collect your test papers from me and wait for me to say 'Start'. The instruction-giver should then continue as follows:
- Wait for 10 seconds and then repeat the instruction but in a more urgent tone.
- Wait for 7 seconds and then re-phrase the instruction.
- Wait for 10 seconds and then deliver each part of the instruction in separate sentences with a pause after each.
- Finally, use gesture to accompany each part of the instruction.
- Stop at this point.

The linguist now tells everyone what the instruction was and then that it was repeated with more urgency, then broken down into shorter instructions and then finally gesture was used. This is typically what we do when we believe the instruction has not been understood. Ask each member of the group how they felt when they did not understand and what they did each time the linguist added more words.

Relate this to the experience of pupils with ASD. While they are processing the first instruction, something else is said in a harsher tone. They do not know which needs more attention. While they are deciding which of the two instructions to pay attention to, something else is said – and so on:

If, as an individual with ASD, you need to dissect every word for its potential meaning and decide on the intention of the speaker and formulate your response you will need more time.

Practice with a partner how long is a comfortable silence between an instruction and the execution. Now try doubling that amount of time to experience how long may need to be given.

Potential skills may need to be broken down into smaller steps and learned one step at a time

- In a small group of three or four people, decide on a particular task or activity – this could be a subject specialist discussion.
- Why might an individual with ASD find this task difficult ?

Continued

- Task analyse the activity into smaller, teachable steps. Decide if it would be better to focus on teaching the final step first (backward chaining) or the first step (forward chaining) ?
- Are there other children who might benefit from having this task in smaller steps too ?

Use visual communication and check that it is understood

- In small groups, decide on an area of the school/classroom that would benefit from more visual information.
- Is it basic school rules – walk in the corridor; pick up a tray before choosing your lunch; rules for using the computer?
- Think of individuals/an individual who needs verbal reminders about a particular expectation.
- Think of their unique characteristics of ASD (e.g. social skills, level of understanding, sensory differences, reactions to verbal reminders) and design a visual way on reinforcing those expectations.
- Discuss how the visual information could be presented to the individual and how to ensure that they have understood the message.

Generalizing skills and understanding

- In pairs or individually, think of a particular concept or skill that the individual with ASD has demonstrated a grasp of.
- What other situations could this be practised in ?
- Who else might be expecting this skill/concept ?
- How can you present the practice in different formats for the individual to generalize ?

Example: Counting in Fives

- In Maths, filling in a hundred square with marking each block of 5 as 5, 10, 15, 20 etc.
- In classroom jobs, counting out pencils, paintbrushes in blocks of 5.
- In stacking chairs, making towers of 5.
- In PE counting how many pupils and making teams of 5.
- In English, 5-line poems (limericks) – how many limericks have a class group made ? How many lines of poetry have been written ?

Recommended reading

Further examples and information can be found in Chapter 2 of Plimley and Publications Bowen (2006a) *Autistic Spectrum Disorders in the Secondary School.* London: Paul Chapman Publishing/ Sage. Practical school provision issues are discussed in a dedicated chapter to this subject. This includes real-life case study information from a teacher who set up a resource base in her school from scratch.

Cumine, V., Leach, J. and Stevenson, G (1998) *Asperger Syndrome – A Practical Guide for Teachers.* London: David Fulton Publishers Ltd. Excellent resource for teachers which looks at whole school approaches to include individuals with Asperger syndrome.

Hanbury, M. (2005) *Educating Pupils with Autistic Spectrum Disorders.* London: Paul Chapman Publishing/Sage Publications. A good resource for staff working with children with Special Educational Needs which covers environmental adaptations for those who cannot function in a typical classroom.

Treatment and Education of Autistic and Communications handicapped Children (TEACCH) uses room management and visual structures to convey expectations of activities – see www.teacch.com

Nguyen, A. (2006) *Creating an Autism-Friendly Environment.* London: NAS. ICAN article gives a brief overview of some considerations relating to environments.

Useful websites

http://www.ican.org.uk/TalkingPoint/Parent%20Point/Communication%20Disability/Conditions%20with%20Communication%20Disability/ASD/Guidleines%20for%20Communicating%20With%20Children%20 with%20ASD/An%20Autism%20Friendly%20Environment.aspx – helpful suggestions for creating a more ASD. friendly environment.

http://www.clubmom.com/display/257510 – Tips from a mother of an individual with ASD.

Try the Ideal Autistic Environment Test at http://iautistic.com/autism-friendly-room-test.php

The NES/NHS Scotland resource for Primary care Practitioners – www.nes.scot.nhs.uk/asd/topics/topic1/sectionc18.htm uses case study examples to look at some environmental issues which may arise on visits to clinics and surgeries.

Opportunities for autism-friendly exercise in NW England – http://www.ucsm.ac.uk/about/news/PR145.php

Look at Autism-friendly school initiatives in Wales – Autism Cymru's Inclusive schools and ASDs training programme – www.awares.org

http://www.autism-friendly.com/latestautismnews.html – information on current ideas and strategies for being autism-friendly. A site from the USA.

Go to the accompanying CD Rom for the full selection of slides that accompany this section and remember you can also access detailed speaker notes to use with each slide.

**Section 6:
CREATING AN ASD–FRIENDLY
ENVIRONMENT**

Implications of Working with Pupils with ASDs

Importance of:
- Understanding psychological functioning
- Understanding challenges to learning faced by the individual with an ASD
- Translate this understanding into effective strategies for teaching and care

Implications

- The principal difficulty for a person with ASDs is that they do not learn in the way that other people do.
- Nor do they perceive the world in the same way
- They may not necessarily have a way into the often social situations where most people learn
- In social interactions that give rise to new learning, the person with ASDs will often have problems

Implications for Staff

- Visual thinkers
- Time to process
- Ability to generalize learning
- Concrete understanding
- Attention to task
- Memory for information
- Sensory issues

Manifested in

- Literality
- Black and white view
- Lack of flexibility
- Inability to read between the lines
- Cannot 'guess' what is needed
- Lack of generalization
- May not recognize non-verbal signals

Whole School Starting Points

- Begin with supporting the individual to be motivated to learn
- Functional environments will mean safety and security
- Adapt to individual strengths and needs and make good use of them
- Motivate, be creative and maintain a belief in your own skills
- Keep your own flexibility and be adaptable

Whole School Starting Points continued

- Understanding ASDs

- Know and use interventions according to the individual and the situation

- Give support where it is needed and often as soon as possible.

- Be willing to learn from and adapt for the pupil

Safe Learning Environments

Features of a 'safe' working environment for individuals with ASDs include :

- Working to promote independence

- Routines and rules that have predictability

- Teaching methods that ensure skills and knowledge are generalized

- Systems and processes that are visually clear

Independence

- Avoid learned helplessness

- Avoid too much verbal prompting

- Always think 'How is this encouraging independence in adult life?'

- Build on identified strengths

- Prioritise short term aims and have an idea of long term aims too

9

Predictability

- Ensure predictability in the physical environment by helping them to:

  – Know where things are

  – Know where activities happen

  – Know what's happening now

  – Know what coming next

10

Clarity

- Give them enough time to process what's being said and to act on it

- Think about breaking down new skills into smaller steps, to be learned one step at a time

- Build up your use of visual communication and make sure that it is understood

- Plan to generalize new skills and learning in different situations/subjects

11

An Enabling Physical Environment

ISSUES TO BEAR IN MIND:

- A noisy classroom may cause distress
- Instructions to the whole class may go over the head
- Having to worry about belongings and furniture may effectively rule out concentration for the whole lesson
- If the teaching medium is oral – the learning medium is auditory – sensory differences may preclude understanding
- Simple instructions may baffle
- The pupil may need a structure within which to function

12

7

Behaviour Management

> ☀ Often, in individuals with ASDs, behaviours can signal distress and anxiety: teachers therefore need to know how to look for potential triggers and examine ways in which problems can be solved from the child's perspective. This section discusses ways in which the individual's behaviour can be understood and how stress levels in pupils and staff can be lowered. It emphasizes the importance of looking at the behaviour from the point of view of the individual with ASD to find a solution.

Rationale

The condition of ASDs and some type of behavioural difficulty is synonymous in the minds of many people. The media portrayal of people with ASD often shows them in times of crises when behaviour can be difficult, destructive or in some way inappropriate. However, there is nothing within the range of behaviours that is evident in the individual with an ASD that is not apparent in the population as a whole. The manifestation of 'unwanted' behaviour is usually as a result of some perceived stressor or a threat to their equilibrium. If we examine how we cope with stress – do we not make repetitive movements, check and recheck that, for instance, the back door is locked, or rock and comfort ourselves when we are very upset?

The term 'challenging behaviour' is a contemporary adjustment away from the view that over-the-top outbursts are the responsibility of their 'owner'. The emphasis is altered to look at the transactional view of the actions as a challenge to us to do something about. Recent work and theory around challenging behaviours (Zarkowska and Clements (1994) and Whitaker (2001)) puts the responsibility on us, as professionals, to examine the reasons for the behaviour and devise a means of counteracting its effects. For the person acting in a 'challenging' way the function of the behaviour might be to secure an escape or to calm them down. Repeated actions of this nature signal a way for them to regain control over a situation by producing a predictable set of responses from us.

For our part, there is a need to act or intervene to defuse 'behaviour'. However, we often act in isolation and therefore there is no continuity of response. So it is imperative that we work together with important people in the individual's life and the person themselves if possible, to teach more socially acceptable alternatives, including being able to articulate the cause of their discomfort.

Behaviourist theories of the 1960s and 1970s advised intervention in the behaviour and the introduction of a consequence that would have an aversive effect on the person (shouting, removal, physical punishment). Current theories realize that it would be a mistake for practitioners to try to extinguish (remove) the behaviour without thinking of teaching an acceptable replacement activity. Many individuals with ASD lack the knowledge to know what they could or should be doing, so the environment that exists on negatives – 'stop that,' 'don't run away,' 'No you can't' does not offer an idea of the acceptable alternative. We need to focus on what we want them to do, rather than what not to do. To punish and/or use aversive practices to respond to the behaviour will only teach the person anxiety/fear and a sense of discomfort. Beware of thinking that an individual who is conforming is also attending, concentrating or understanding what is needed. We tend to view conformity as a positive quality, but conformity can be a learned behaviour – if being quiet, looking at the teacher and sitting still is valued, the individual with ASDs may do that in order to avoid further stress. It is a mistake to think that they are attending and learning at the same time.

Current strategies/interventions carefully examine and interpret the function of the behaviour for the person. Most behaviour gives out a message and by looking at the underlying 'message', we are moving towards finding an acceptable replacement for it.

Useful resources

Stress relief

Look at a case study written for Primary Care Practitioners which could be used as an additional training resource – http://www.nes.scot.nhs.uk/asd/scenarios/jake.htm

Biofeedback – there are a number of biofeedback devices that can be used to help the individuals with ASDs to monitor their own stress levels and aid relaxation. A fantasy adventure programme called 'Journey to the Wild Divine,' links feedback via the fingertips to a series of screens on a computer where the progress towards relaxation results in actions in the adventure. This has been trialled in a secondary school and has proved successful with some pupils. See www.wilddivine.com. See also the article by Gary Ames (2006) – http://www.alertfocus.com/relieve/autism/newvisions.php? PHPSESSID= e088dbdad9ddad997caea75cbfe2638a.

Other ways of promoting self-management of levels of arousal are the use of heart rate monitors which are popular in the world of athletics and sport. A low restrictive device, such as a polar heart rate monitor can help the individual to watch their heart rate and use calming techniques that they have been taught to bring down high levels. See http://www.heartratemonitor.co.uk/

Recognizing and forewarning of stress levels

Use of a visual system to denote positive and negative behaviours using red (negative) and green (positive) cards can help individuals with ASDs learn to manage their behaviours. See website: www.redandgreenchoices.com or read: Green, Irene (2003) *Red and Green Choices – A Positive Behavioural Developmental Strategy*, available via the website or from P.O. Box 5, Huron, Ohio 44839, USA

Visual systems that indicate stress

Traffic light systems

The teacher/support worker either uses a visible traffic light system of cards to indicate when behaviour is acceptable (green). Or the individual can have asset of cards to indicate clearly by placing the coloured card on their table when, their stress levels are calm (green) getting too much (amber) or they are about to 'blow' (red).

See also http://www.proteacher.net/archive/posts/2002/07/25/43731.html for a whole class idea of using a traffic light system.

Stress bucket

Use the strongly visual idea of having a 'Stress bucket.' Teacher/support worker have their own bucket (preferably transparent) and marbles or beads are put into the bucket as their stress levels rise. This could be adopted by the individual with ASD, so that those around them can clearly see when their stress levels are beginning to rise. The levels can go down too! See http://www.shapeup.org/about/arch_news/nl1006.html for further de-stressing ideas for individuals with ASD.

 Case studies

The following case studies present some typical behaviour scenarios that may occur in different settings. Each case study is followed up by questions that seek to elicit what the possible cause of the behaviour is and what the behaviour might be 'saying'.

Continued

Home – Winston aged 4

Winston really does not like any visitors coming to his home. He always reacts in an over-the-top way and will run upstairs and hide in his bedroom. Only when he hears the front door closing and the visitors leaving, will he come out of his room without a fuss. His family have tried to make him stay in the room with other people but he screams and cries and will start throwing ornaments if he cannot escape. They have a large family who do like to call in to see them whenever they are in the area.

- What needs checking on when and why this behaviour occurs ? What might the message in the behaviour be ?

Early Years – Sophie aged 3

Sophie will not sit on the carpet for storytime. She actively resists bending her knees to sit down and if there are others nearby she will lash out at them. The only time she will sit and listen to the story is if she is sitting on the edge of the lino by herself.

- What needs checking on when and why this behaviour occurs ? What might the message in the behaviour be ?

Primary – Danuta aged 7

Danuta always loses it when she has completed one piece of work and her teacher or LSA (learning support assistant) asks her to do another page. This is at its most acute during maths when, because of her good ability, she often finishes before her peers.

- What needs checking on when and why this behaviour occurs ? What might the message in the behaviour be ?

Secondary – Stefan aged 15

Stefan always has a major 'meltdown' when he has a supply teacher. He has developed a good relationship with most of his subject teachers and can work independently in most academic lessons. Once he enters the room and sees that it is not the teacher he is expecting, then he becomes loud and verbally abusive and has to leave the room.

- What needs checking on when and why this behaviour occurs ? What might the message in the behaviour be ?

Special – Dafydd aged 13

Dafydd usually copes with the canteen-style lunchtime. He has his own place to sit and is with supportive peers and a member of staff. He can be relied on to have good table manners and he helps to tidy the dining room after everyone has gone. A new child has been promoted to help with the clearing away duties and the first time this happened Dafydd, started to throw the chairs and had to be removed. He hasn't helped since then and his behaviour at the dining table has deteriorated.

- What needs checking on when and why this behaviour occurs ? What might the message in the behaviour be ?

Residential – Errol aged 17

Errol has developed a curiosity in girls which may be related to his own puberty. He has tried to feel their breasts and lift their skirts when they walk past. Members of staff have been told to counter this behaviour by shouting 'No Errol ! Stop that !' If he persists he is taken to his room as a punishment. Some members of staff are amused by this behaviour and have been known to laugh and joke instead of intervening.

- What needs checking on when and why this behaviour occurs ? What might the message in the behaviour be ?

Continued

Young Adult – Miriam aged 21

Miriam has started supported employment in a firm of accountants. She does office duties of filing, tidying, photocopying and making the tea. A member of staff recently tidied up the kitchen and also re-arranged the drawers in the filing cabinets in chronological, rather than alphabetical order. This has upset Miriam and she spends the day verbally checking if she has put the filing away in the right place. Staff feel she is demanding too much support and are asking if she is in the right job.

- What needs checking on when and why this behaviour occurs ? What might the message in the behaviour be?

 ## Extension activities

These activities can be used with small groups to look ways in which behaviour can be recorded, monitored and interpreted. The focus will be on an individual known to the group, rather than a fictitious case study, so therefore, the activity could fulfil an in-house problem-solving role.

Activity 1

Divide into three groups and analyse a real case of inappropriate or unwanted behaviour:
- Group 1 using Whitaker's 8-step plan
- Group 2 using a STAR (Settings, Trigger, Action and Response) approach
- Group 3 using ABC (Antecedents. Behaviour and Consequences).

Share the results of each analysis and have a discussion on what each system yields in terms of information. What is the whole group's decision on the most informative system ?
Develop an action plan of adopting the chosen system of analysis.

Activity 2

- Do an analysis with a partner of an occasion when you or they have been very stressed or upset.
- Look at Whitaker's prompts and see if you can re-work the outcome of your reaction.
- Discuss what works best for you to defuse stress and anxiety.

Activity 3

- Do an audit of reward systems in your establishment.
- Discuss how rewards are differentiated according to your knowledge of the individual. How can rewards be made more individualized ?
- What are the constraints in your setting that go against the opportunity of the individual with an ASD pursuing their special interest as a reward ?
- Now extend the discussion to looking at teaching the individual acceptable forms of stress relief.

Recommended reading

Cumine, V., Leach, J. and Stevenson, G (1998) *Asperger Syndrome – A Practical Guide for Teachers.* London: David Fulton Publishers Ltd. This gives a comprehensive overview of Asperger syndrome (AS) and a series of case studies where 'looking through an Asperger's lens' has helped others to interpret the behaviour of an individual with AS.

Plimley, L.A. and Bowen, M. (2006) *Autistic Spectrum Disorders in the Secondary School.* London: Paul Chapman Publishing. This and the following title have further information and strategies for managing inappropriate behaviour.

Plimley, L.A. and Bowen, M. (2007) *Autistic Spectrum Disorders in the Early Years.* London: Paul Chapman Publishing.

Sainsbury, C. (2000) *A Martian in the Playground.* Bristol: Lucky Duck Green. The perspective of a first person author is always illuminating and gives good insights into how inappropriate behaviour is almost always a communication to others,

Whitaker, P. (2001) *Challenging Behaviour and Autism. Making Sense – Making Progress.* London: National Autistic Society. This gives the background and further detail to the 8-step plan.

Zarkowska, E. and Clements, J. (1994) *Problem Behaviour and People with Severe Learning Difficulties.* London: Chapman and Hall. This gives the background and further detail to the STAR approach.

Useful websites

http://www.nes.scot.nhs.uk/asd/scenarios/jake.htm

www.wilddivine.com

http://www.alertfocus.com/relieve/autism/newvisions.php?
  PHPSESSID=e088dbdad9ddad997caea75cbfe2638a

http://www.heartratemonitor.co.uk/

www.redandgreenchoices.com

http://www.proteacher.net/archive/posts/2002/07/25/43731.html

http://www.shapeup.org/about/arch_news/nl1006.html

Donna Williams poetry on behaviour – http://www.donnawilliams.net/respect.0.html

For Wendy Lawson – http://mugsy.org/wendy/

 Go to the accompanying CD-Rom for the full selection of slides that accompany this section and remember you can also access detailed speaker notes to use with each slide.

Section 7:
BEHAVIOUR MANAGEMENT

1

Behaviour

- All behaviour has message value (La Vigna and Donnellan, 1986)

- Behaviour can result from a combination of personality and context

- Nobody can begin to learn if they are permanently at breaking point

Source: La Vigna, G. W. & Donnellan, A. M. (1986) *Alternatives to Punishment: Solving Behaviour Problems with Non-aversive Strategies.* New York: Irvington Publishers.

2

Melt Down

'Temple Grandin has compared "melt downs" to epileptic fits, which can't be stopped once they have been started, but must be allowed to run their course. It is best to see what's going on as "brainstorm" rather than some one not being able to control themselves or having a tantrum.'

Source: Sainsbury, C. (2000) *Martian in the Playground*, London: Lucky Duck/ Paul Chapman Publishing.

3

Strategies: Asperger's Lens

'In order to intervene in an attempt to change the behaviour of children with Asperger syndrome, it is first necessary to understand the function or purpose of the behaviour–*from the point of view of the child.* It is important to look at the behaviour and events surrounding it, as if through an "Asperger's lens".'

Source: Cumine, V. Leach, J. and Stevenson, G. (1998) *Asperger Syndrome – A Practical Guide for Teachers.* London: David Fulton Publishers Ltd.

4

Case Study

SAM: Sam continuously rolls a pencil rapidly and noisily between his hands– distracting the other children in his primary class.

THEORY: Use obsession as a reward, rather than trying to eliminate it.

Source: Cumine, V. Leach, J. and Stevenson, G. (1998) *Asperger Syndrome – A Practical Guide for Teachers.* London: David Fulton Publishers Ltd.

5

Case Study continued

Original intervention:

Had the aim of eliminating the pencil rolling behaviour. Rewards were offered but were ineffective.

6

Whitaker's Eight Step Plan
(Whitaker, 2001)

- Deciding where to start
- Pinpointing the settings
- Looking for triggers
- Results-what happens next?
- Meaning-what's it all about?
- Prevention
- New skills and behaviour
- Changing the results

Source: Whitaker, P. (2001) *Challenging behaviour and Autism. Making Sense – Making Progress.* London: National Autistic Society.

7

Case Study continued

What would the Asperger's lens show?

- Pencil rolling behaviour obsessional
- To some extent it is necessary

New Intervention

- Use pencil rolling as a reward
- Sam allowed to roll pencil in transition, when children moving and are noisier

8

Where to Start

- List behaviour that concerns you
- Is it a danger?
- Does it interfere with ability to learn?
- Does it restrict access?
- How much stress and for whom?
- How frequent and intense?
- Focus and keep a record

9

Pinpointing the Setting

- When, where and with whom the problem occurs
- What the child should be doing
- The child's emotional state
- When the problem does *not* happen – a big clue to the trigger

10

Looking for Triggers

- Does someone make a demand?
- Does something make a demand?
- Is the trigger something your child suddenly notices or pays attention to (even when nothing in the situation has changed)
- Could the trigger be something that happens when the child does not expect it to?
- Exceptions to the rule

11

What happens next?

- Child could be just interested in making something happen
- The behaviour may create physical or sensory results
- What are the reactions of other?
- Something might stop happening after the behaviour, e.g. people reducing demands

12

What's it all About?

- Is the behaviour telling you something about the child's feelings?
- Is the behaviour a means of escape?
- Is the behaviour a way of getting what the child needs – object, activity, stimulation, contact, attention?

13

Prevention

- Can some of the settings and triggers be avoided?
- Is there a way to reduce demands?
- Can settings and triggers be altered? Would more structure help? Do expectations need to be more explicit? Can you give advance warning?
- What can you learn from settings where the problem does not occur?

14

New Skills and Behaviour

- What do you want him to be doing at times when he is behaving in a difficult way?
- What skills might help him cope with the problem?
- How could he get some better pay offs?

15

Changing the Results

- How do we encourage behaviour we want to see?
- How can a replacement behaviour achieve better results?
- Can we find a way to stop the behaviour resulting in pay off so that motivation to behave in this way is reduced?

16

Strategies for Improving Behaviour

- Rules are very important: Temple Grandin lives by a set of rules.

- Advanced preparation of change in routine

- Calm, neutral approaches to negotiation

- Incorporate special interests into programme and make preferred activities a reward

- Have a special calming–down room

17

Strategies continued

- Reward and praise appropriate behaviour

- Provide clear boundaries and targets

- Disapprove of the behaviour not the child

- Tell the child what to do rather that not what to do

- Be consistent and sensitive

- Give pupils a responsible role

18

Pupil Participation and Peer Group Awareness

Just like other pupils, those with ASDs will need to be provided with opportunites to participate in decision-making processes, especially those decisions that directly affect them. Pupils with ASDs should be encouraged to take an active part in school life through social skills groups, reviews, transition planning meetings and school councils. It is important to note that in some cases there may be a need for an advocacy service or additional support.

It is important that neurotypical pupils in schools respect individual differences and understand that ASD is a hidden disability. This section will also give a brief overview of how such awareness raising might happen.

Rationale

Pupil participation

Governments in the UK are fully committed to the recommendations set out in the United Nations Convention on the Rights of the Child. This is reflected in legislation and documentation, such as *Every Child Matters* (DfES, 2003) and *Rights to Action. Implementing Children and Young People's Rights in Wales* (WAG, 2007). This dedication is also reflected in the appointment of Children's Commissioners across the UK countries. With regard to children and young people with Special Educational Needs, the Codes of Practice in England and Wales both have a section dedicated to pupil participation.

Pupils can participate on a number of levels. Hart (1992) suggests that consultation is one of the many methods of participation. His 'ladder' of participation ranges from 'manipulative' and 'decorative' at the bottom to child initiated projects and sharing decision-making with adults at the top. Treseder's (1997) model of participation moves away from the notion of the ladder and recognizes that different approaches may be best in different circumstances. His degrees of participation include:

- Consulted and informed – the project is run by adults but children are consulted.
- Assigned but informed – Adults choose the project and children volunteer. They know who decided to involve them and why.
- Child initiated, shared decisions with adults – children set up the project but take advice and support from adults.
- Child initiated and directed – Young people have the idea and run with the project. Adults are available but do not take charge.
- Adult initiated, shared decisions with adults – Adults have the initial idea but children are involved in the planning and decision-making.

Much work still needs to be done in developing the skills and confidence of adults to ensure that they can appropriately support children and young people to participate.

Schools need to have demonstrable evidence that information gained from pupils has been used to influence school policy and practice. Pupils should be able to see clearly how their input to decision-making has impacted either their own progress or solved a problem. They must be given feedback in this respect. Schools will need to provide pupils with user friendly information so that they can understand the subject matter, the purpose and the process. For pupils with ASDs, such information will need to be clearly written, unambiguous and contain visual cues.

Children and young people with ASDs can be encouraged to influence their own learning outcomes by getting involved in target-setting, IEPs (Individual Education Plans), Reviews and Transition Planning. Parts of the curriculum, e.g. Personal and Social Education can be used to develop the skills and self-confidence required to become an active participant in school life.

It may be necessary for schools to create a checklist or a set of quality standards in relation to pupil participation.

Useful resources

The following resources offer examples of how school staff might encourage pupil participation. They can also be freely downloaded from the Internet.

- The SEN Toolkit was produced by DfES and contains practical advice on how to implement the Code of Practice. It should be read in conjunction with the Code. Each section of the Toolkit has a number of pages designed to be copied and used for training purposes. Section 4 deals with 'Enabling Participation.' Available from www.teachernet.gov.uk/wholeschool/sen/sentoolkit/
- The Welsh Assembly Government (WAG, 2002) has produced a *Handbook of Good Practice for Children with Special Educational Needs* to accompany the *Code of Practice* in Wales. Section 3 examines pupil participation and provides some advice on useful strategies. A number of materials and case study examples can be found in the appendices. This is available from www.learning.wales.gov.uk
- Although not aimed at children and young people with additional learning needs, yet *The Evaluator's Cook Book Participatory Evaluation Exercises* (NECF/KatalystTales, 2005) is an ideal resource for those working with pupils with ASDs. The National Evaluation of the Children's Fund (NECF) has adopted a range of participatory evaluation techniques with children and young people. The 'Cook Book' brings together a range of approaches in a clear and simple format. It is divided into three main sections:
  - Starters – short warm-up exercises
  - Main courses – more substantial exercises which give children and young people the opportunity to creatively explore the issues in their lives, and
  - Puddings – shorter exercises to 'round off' and evaluate sessions with participants. This wonderful resource is available from http://www.everychildmatters.gov.uk/_files/08855CC339C76D2C7C11A0 C4830317FB.pdf
- The WAG *Strategic Action Plan for Wales – ASDs* is a consultation document in an ASD-user-friendly format and is downloadable in PDF from www.awares.org
- *The Training Activities Toolkit* consists of a series of activities to help staff and pupils set up and develop an effective school council. The activities have been differentiated for use with pupils with additional learning needs and can be used to encourage pupil participation in a number of ways. The Toolkit is available in the section for professionals and governors on www.schoolcouncilswales.org.uk/en/fe/page_at.asp?n1=30& n2=34&n3=87

Case studies

These case study examples can be used to facilitate discussion across the age range. At all times participants should be encouraged to reflect upon whether or not their suggestions are tokenistic or really do offer an opportunity for genuine participation.

Early Years – Jennie aged 5

Jennie is five-years-old. She is reluctant to communicate but can use picture symbols to express her needs. Jennie has her own folder containing the picture symbols and will use

Continued

the symbols with adult prompting. This usually happens at break or lunchtime, but not so often during the rest of the school day. What strategies can be put in place to give Jennie opportunities to make choices throughout the school day?

 Issues to consider

- Jennie will be confused by too much choice so classroom staff need to keep the activity very simple.
- Jennie can continue to be given a choice of two drinks and two foods using her picture symbols at breaktime. She may need some physical prompting to do this. Also it may be necessary to show her the actual drinks and foods to make a choice.
- Jennie can be encouraged to make a choice of a drink or a pudding at lunchtime if she does not bring a packed lunch to school. Many children with ASDs will prefer a packed lunch if they have unusual preferences in food.
- Jennie may find breaktimes and lunchtimes stressful – lots of movement and noise. If she has a favourite activity or 'special interest' that she could do in a quiet place, school staff could provide her with the opportunity to choose to do this.
- Jennie could be encouraged to make a choice of classroom activity at certain times during the day, e.g. water play or art using picture symbols. It is important not to force Jennie into participating in an activity which, because of the sensory issues, she may find stressful, e.g. sand, clay, hand painting etc.

 Case studies

Primary – Tommy aged 7

Tommy is seven-years-old. He gets very distressed at the end of the day during story time. At this time children are expected to sit on the carpet and listen carefully. Tommy does not have a very good idea about personal space and tends to sit far too close to children and this causes annoyance to both him and them. He also complains bitterly that the feel of the carpet makes him feel itchy all over. How would you manage this situation?

 Issues to consider

- Sensory anomalies might mean that Tommy finds the situation extremely uncomfortable. ASD is a disability, and, as for other children with sensory or physical disability, allowances will need to be made. This is his right.
- Teachers may use the argument that we cannot treat children differently but if inclusion is going to work and we are going to really listen to children then sometimes this may need to happen. It may well be better for all concerned if during storytime, Tommy is allowed to sit on a chair close to the group. The other children may appreciate the fact that he is not invading their personal space and everyone will be able to enjoy the story without distraction.

Case studies

Secondary – Ahmed age 13

Ahmed is thirteen-years-old and often interrupts during a class debate, giving other youngsters little time to contribute to the discussion. What can you do to make sure everyone can have their say?

 Issues to consider

- Social skills groups and social use of language programmes, such as SULP (Rinaldi,1993) can be useful in teaching pupils with ASDs the rules of turn taking in a conversation. Remember this skill will not come naturally to Ahmed.
- Ahmed can be given a rule. The class rule can be no one can speak for more than three minutes in a class discussion and everyone must allow two other people to speak before they speak again. An egg timer can be used to time pupils' talk time and Ahmed can use a ticking system to count when he is allowed to speak again.

 Case studies

Young Adult – Gerson aged 15

Gerson is due to leave school for further education in 12 months time. How can you make sure that he plays an active part in transition planning so that his needs are fully met when he leaves school?

 Issues to consider

- Gerson must play an active part in transition planning including being supported to write his own action plans.
- Gerson should be encouraged to make up a portfolio of strengths, but also areas of difficulty, that he can share with new staff in advance of the move.
- Gerson should be given the opportunity to visit college on a number of occasions. He should especially be given the opportunity to see what college is like at mealtimes, breaktimes and during lesson changes. He should be encouraged to discuss his concerns following this opportunity and invited to say what he will need to make potentially stressful times easier for him.

 Extension activities

The following activities can help participants explore issues around participation in more detail. We recommend that you use an appropriate case study example and one or two of the extension activities.

Continued

- Ask participants to get into small groups and make a list of all the ways in which they think they encourage and invite pupil participation. Ask them to honestly think about whether they work in an environment that has shared ownership involving staff, pupils, parents and the wider community. Ask each group to name two things they do that demonstrate this. Record on a flip chart and circulate after the meeting.
- Write a range of statements related to children's rights and pupil participation on laminated card. Examples might include 'All children must be treated equally', 'Children should have the right to stay in the classrooms at breaktimes if they wish'. Make sure the statements are contentious and slightly ambiguous. Make two or three sets of the cards (up to 10 statements) and ask participants to discuss each in turn and rank on a continuum of whether they agree or disagree. At the end of the session, give the groups an opportunity to feed back to the wider group.
- Prepare a short true-or-false quiz based on all the relevant legislation and documentation related to participation. For example, focus on *Every Child Matters* (England) or *Children and Young People: Rights to Action* (Wales).
- Ask participants to consider a pupil with ASD who they are working with. What barriers need to be overcome to enable active participation in decision-making?
- Provide groups with materials and activities set out in *The Cook Book*. Ask each group to select an issue for discussion and get them to role play how they think this activity might work in the classroom.

Recommended reading

The following texts can be recommended as additional reading following the training session. Some of them focus on the *Every Child Matters* agenda and can be downloaded freely from the internet. Some focus on participation and Additional Learning Needs rather than on ASDs specifically but they are nevertheless useful in demonstrating the difference between true participation and tokenism.

Children and Young People's Unit (2001) *Learning to Listen. Core Principles for the Involvement of Children and Young People,* available from www.everychildmatters.gov.uk/participation/buildingaculture. This government publication outlines the importance of listening to children and young people.

Fajeman, L. and Treseder, P. (2002) *Children are Service Users Too?* London: Save the Children. This publication is the result of research undertaken into value of children commenting on the services they must use.

Jelly, M. et al. (2000) *Involving Pupils in Practice. Promoting Partnerships with Pupils with Special Educational Needs.* London: David Fulton. This generic text examines issues around pupil empowerment, self-esteem, leadership, learning styles and collaboration. It contains photocopiable materials.

MacCornville, R. (2007) *Looking at Inclusion. Listening to the Voices of Young People.* Bristol: Lucky Duck Books. This book covers a wider range of disabilities including ASDs. It demonstrates how eliciting pupils' views can lead to successful inclusion. It contains case studies, practical strategies and information about useful resources.

National Children's Bureau/PK Research Consultancy (2003) *Handbook: Building a Culture of Participation,* available from www.everychildmatters.gov.uk/participation/buildingaculture. Another government publication that offers advice and guidance on the *Every Child Matters* agenda.

Treseder, P. (1997) *Empowering Children and Young People Training Manual: Promoting Involvement in Decision Making.* London: Save the Children. Treseder examines the difference between tokenism and true participation. His model of degrees of participation can serve as a useful audit tool.

Useful websites

www.everychildmatters.gov.uk/participation
www.everychildmatters.gov.uk/participation/buildingaculture
www.ncb.org.uk
www.dfes.gov.uk/cypu
www.nch.org.uk
www.wales.gov.uk
www.dfes.gov.uk/sen
www.funkydragon.org
www.crae.org.uk

www.participationworks.org.uk
www.nya.org.uk
www.aspiesforfreedom.com
http://ani.autistics.org
www.schoolcouncilswales.org.uk

 Go to the accompanying CD-Rom, for the full selection of slides that accompany this section and remember you can also access detailed speaker notes to use with each slide.

Section 8:

PUPIL PARTICIPATION
AND
PEER GROUP AWARENESS

Pupil Participation

- The United Nations Convention on the Rights of the Child gives children a set of economic, social, cultural, civil and political rights

- It was UK ratified in December 1991

Other Relevant Legislation

- One of five outcomes of children's well being in the Children Act 2004 is 'making a positive contribution'

- Regulations passed by Parliament in 2003 allow children and young people to become 'associate members' of a committee of a school governing body

Relevant Legislation

- Every Child Matters

- National Service Framework for Children, Young People and Maternity Services

- SENDA

Relevant Legislation continued

- Section 7 of the Education Act 2005 requires school inspectors (Ofsted/Estyn) to have regard to the views of students when carrying out school inspections

- The Special Educational Needs Code of Practice in England and Wales recognizes the importance of pupil involvement

Non Participation

- Manipulation

- Decoration

- Tokenism

Effective Participation

- Listening to pupil

- Supporting pupils to express their views

- Taking views into account

- Involving pupils in decision–making process

- Sharing power and responsibility for decision making

Funky Dragon's List

- Showing respect
- Involving us in deciding/organizing what when where
- Making sure adults don't take over
- Having fun
- Making activities/consultation user friendly
- Paying attention and taking notes
- Liaising with decision–makers
- Letting us know what is going on
- Talking afterwards and explaining things

Facilitating Participation

- Pastoral Support Groups

- School and Class Councils

- Social Skills Groups

- Circle of Friends

9

Opportunities

- Setting learning targets

- Contributing to IEPs and Reviews

- Contributing to Assessment of Need

- Transition Planning

- Peer Review

- Roles of Responsibility

10

Curriculum

- Thinking Skills

- Communication

- Personal and Social Education

11

Peer Group awareness

- Some tried and tested strategies use peer group awareness of ASDs as a starting point to targeting effective peer support
- 'Circle of Friends' is one such strategy
- Peers of the individual with ASDs are encouraged to reflect upon positive qualities within themselves and others
- The adult facilitator asks for volunteers to form a 'Circle of Friends' for an individual in need of support

12

What makes a Circle ?

- Peers volunteer to become part of a circle

- An adult facilitates and takes their lead from the pupils

- They meet regularly to act as a resource for a 'focus' pupil

- The outcome is mutually positive and supportive

13

Key Components of Effective Friendships (Gold, 1999)

- a climate of acceptance, not judgement

- mutual liking

- positive pro-disability attitudes

- friendships are not just 1:1

- teenage years are the time when a separation develops from parents and families and reliance and dependence is created around our peers

Source: Gold, D. (1999) 'Friendship, leisure and support: The purposes of 'Circles of Friends' of young people', *Journal of Leisurability*, 26.3.

14

What are the Optimum Conditions for an Effective Circle ?

- 6–8 volunteer members
- opportunity to meet regularly (once per week)
- meetings of around 20–30 minutes
- 5 main aims
    – to create a support network for the focus pupil
    – to offer encouragement
    – to identify strategies to achieve targets
    – to put the strategies into continuous use
    – to recognize progress and success

15

Listing the Positives

- A piece of research by Leicestershire Outreach Team finds that volunteers have great insight into the strengths of others
- They can be inventive about 'special interests' being turned into valued skills
- They can give credit to the focus pupil's idiosyncrasies
- Lists of positives were consistently longer than negatives

16

Listing the Negatives

- Facilitators need to be mindful of not being drawn into an alliance of disapproval or colluding with a group's norms
- It is important and can be a relief to give a voice to their misgivings/misunderstandings
- Their concerns are being taken seriously by an adult
- They may be relieved to find 'It's not just me' amongst their peers
- The 'mad or bad' perception of some behaviours will be shifted into a proactive realm

17

Other Ideas

'It is hard to have great self-esteem when you are the one who is always being helped'

Jim Sinclair, a man with ASDs

As part of peer awareness, it is important to identify the skills and strengths of the individual and how they can help others

The inclusive teacher will look for ways to use the skills of the individual with ASDs

18

How can the Support be Reciprocal ?

Kluth (2003) suggests the following :–

- Find partners in activities in which the individual with ASDs can act as mentor
- Encourage the person to publicize their interests or skills – a ready-made talking point
- Use the individual to assist those in need of support in a topic/subject they excel in – e.g. IT support
- Offer clubs and after school activities to extend their strengths, maybe with older children

Source: Kluth, P. (2003) *You're Gonna Love this Kid.* Marlyand: Paul H Brookes.

19

Community Building Activities

Suggestions from Kluth (2003) for more inclusive practices:

- Group résumé – acknowledges skills of whole group
- Pass the compliment – positive feedback
- A truth or a lie – 3 written statements – 2 true and 1 a lie – pair up to problem solve to find the lie
- Paper bag interviews – questions posted into a paper bag, small groups draw out questions and answer them one by one

Source: Kluth, P. (2003) *You're Gonna Love this Kid.* Marlyand: Paul H Brookes.

20

Keep the Individual at the Heart of the Community

- True inclusion respects the needs and strengths of all
- The individual with ASD needs to be at the centre of inclusive activity, not on the fringes
- Adults need to be models of anti–discriminatory attitudes and practices
- Inclusion is best started with the very young and then progressed through life

21

Working with Parents and Other Professionals

> This section will focus on issues around multi-agency and multi-disciplinary working and the importance of developing effective methods of communication and defining roles and responsibilities. The final part of the presentation will suggest ways in which schools can effectively communicate with home via newsletters, meetings, information points, home–school diaries.

A successful service is based on a team of dedicated individuals working together. Ideally this team will consist of representatives from many disciplines. For instance, the current recommendations for the assessment and diagnosis of ASDs (National Initiative for Autism, 2003) are that a multi-disciplinary team of professionals, such as education staff, educational/clinical psychology, speech and language therapy and medical professionals should work together to gather observational and assessment data as a team. Team working, particularly across disciplines, can be difficult to arrange and manage. Often practices and processes differ enormously between education, social services and health, sometimes the language used can be subject to misinterpretation amongst professionals. Professionals involved in the care and education of individuals with ASDs bear a responsibility to communicate and collaborate with each other for the benefit of the individual. Where it comes to communicating and working with parents, then it is absolutely paramount. Attfield and Morgan (2006) say that families need to know the results of assessment and diagnosis as early as possible, so that they can assimilate the information and mobilize follow-up support. They need a continuous dialogue with professionals so that, as they grow in their knowledge and understanding, there can be further discussions on how to care for their child.

Many parents report feeling bereaved and enter a period of grief upon the diagnosis of ASDs. Parents need time and space to work through the range of feelings that accompany a bereavement – guilt, denial, anxiety, despondency – before they feel strong enough to think and act proactively. Teams of professionals need to listen to the parents and respect their emotions, however painful they may be. Services are developing the idea of having a 'key' professional who works directly with the parents (recommended in the *Strategic Action Plan for Wales*, WAG, 2007), so that one key person is there to support the parents and will filter all information through to them. If a family is working through the stages of grief, then they are not going to feel emotionally or intellectually strong enough to face a barrage of requests, information and appointments from the list of professionals indicated above.

This section offers guidance on procedures for effective collaboration. It will give an overview of the legal requirements in terms of parent partnerships and how schools can be part of a joined up network of support and information for parents and carers. The availability of different types of good practice guidance since 2002 can be used as a catalyst in opening discussions with local agencies and support services. The *Every Child Matters* agenda promotes more seamless working between everyone involved in the care of children, parents included. National initiatives on behalf of Scotland, Wales and Northern Ireland will assist all professionals in building true parent partnerships.

Useful resources

Useful Associations for ASD

Autism Cymru – www.awares.org
Autism Initiatives – www.autisminitiatives.org
Autism Northern Ireland – www.autismni.org
Autism Republic of Ireland – http://wwww.oil.ie/~isa1/
Autism West Midlands – www.autismwestmidlands.org.uk
National Autistic Society – www.nas.org
Scottish Society for Autism – www.autism-in-scotland.org.uk

Case studies

Early Years – Paolo aged 3

Paolo has just started nursery. He spends most of his time tucked inside a blanket in the home corner. His parents want to know how he is progressing and if he talks at much at nursery as he does at home. Staff at the nursery are not sure what to say to them.

What would be a good starting point to open up a dialogue with parents?

Primary – Mohammed aged 8

Mohammed's parents are concerned that although he is progressing well in school, yet when he gets home from school he is overactive and this persists through the night. His father works shifts at nights, which means the main child care falls on his mother. Both parents want to know what approaches work well in school and want to try and replicate this at home.

A meeting is set up – what information will be shared with them?

Secondary – Adrianna aged 11

Adrianna has not managed the transition to secondary school well. Her glowing reports from year 6 are not born out in her current school performance. Adrianna is struggling for the first time in her academic subjects, has difficulties with social demands during the school day and is being teased and singled out by her year 7 peers. This is causing concern for parents and staff who feel she may be on the autistic spectrum.

What are the first steps to be taken towards assessing whether it is ASD?

Young Adult – Siobhan aged 18

Siobhan has got the grades she needs to go onto the university of her choice to study music. She has ASD but is very able academically. Her parents are worried that she will not cope with the geographical/physical layout of the university and she has not declared her disability on her admission forms, so they fear she will not get help in at least settling into university life.

How can they broach potential problems with her tutors?

Residential – Angus aged 14

Angus is at a rural residential college. He has some physical co-ordination difficulties but is eager to go on the overnight camp which will form part of his Duke of Edinburgh Award. Staff also have concerns about his ability to manage the cross-country walk, setting up camp and being independent in his own care.

What should be their first move in assessing his suitability for the activity?

Extension activities

Ways in which this training material can be extended are going to vary according to setting. The following is a broad range of suggestions of how those working with individuals with ASDs and their families can become more familiar with the legal responsibilities of their work; can measure their current practice against a good practice audit tool; and use their own internal audit to inform how their partnerships with parents are currently working.

- If this section forms part of ongoing training, then participants could be encouraged to find all of the relevant pieces of legislation and guidance mentioned in Section 9.
- An audit of your service's move towards developing an Accessibility Plan and Disability Equality Scheme may help to give pointers and an action plan.
- Use one of the Good Practice Guidance tools to audit the understanding, knowledge and provision for individuals with ASD in your school – what are the areas in need of improvement?
- Check the access information/arrangements for contacting all of the other agencies involved in the life of the individual with ASD. Check if there is a local area co-ordination group for ASD in your area.
- Look at ways in which parents could be encouraged into your school more.
- Look at how your school communicates with parents – does it encourage their participation ? How could it be improved?
- Work with colleagues on developing a plan for being a 'welcoming school'.

Recommended reading

The following texts appear in the introduction to this section and are given for readers/ trainers to find further information on this topic.

Attfield, E. and Morgan, H. (2006) *Living with Autistic Spectrum Disorders*. London: Sage/Paul Chapman Publications.

National Initiative for Autism: Screening and Assessment (NIASA) (2003) *National Autism Plan for Children. NAP-C: Plan for the Identification, Assessment and Diagnosis of Children with ASDs.* London: National Autistic Society.

Welsh Assembly Government (2007) *Strategic Action Plan for Wales - ASDs.*

Useful websites

The *SEN Toolkit* was produced by DfES and contains practical advice on how to implement the *Code of Practice*. It should be read in conjunction with the Code. Each section of the Toolkit has a number of pages designed to be copied and used for training purposes. Section 4 deals with 'Enabling Participation'. Available from www.teachernet.gov/wholeschool/sen/

Although not aimed at children and young people with additional learning needs, *Yet The Evaluator's Cook Book: Participatory Evaluation Exercises* (NECF/KatalystTales, 2005) is an ideal resource for those working with pupils with ASDs. See www.everychildmatters.gov.uk/participation/buildingaculture/

The WAG Strategic Action Plan for ASDs consultation document in an ASD-user-friendly format and is downloadable in PDF from www.awares.org Advisory Centre for Education – ACE – http://www.ace-ed.org.uk/ Centre for Studies on Inclusive Education (CSIE) – http://inclusion.uwe.ac.uk/csie

Contact a family – www.cafamily.org.uk

Education Otherwise – www.education-otherwise.org

National Association for Special Educational Needs – www.nasen.org

Network 81 – www.network81.co.uk

OAASIS – www.oaasis.co.uk

Parent Partnership schemes – type the words 'parent partnership scheme' and the name of your local town/authority into the search engine and local information will come up.

Pre-school learning alliance – www.pre-school.org
www.everychildmatters.gov.uk/participation

www.everychildmatters.gov.uk/participation/buildingaculture
www.ncb.org.uk
www.wales.gov.uk
www.dfes.gov.uk/sen
www.funkydragon.org
www.participationworks.org.uk
www.nya.org.uk
www.niccy.org
www.schoolscouncilswales.org.uk

 Go to the accompanying CD-Rom, for the full selection of slides that accompany this section and remember you can also access detailed speaker notes to use with each slide.

Section 9:

**WORKING WITH PARENTS
AND
OTHER PROFESSIONALS**

1

Working with Parents and Other Professionals - Overview

- The parent's view

- Legal requirements upon services

- The statutory framework

- Working in partnership with parents

- Multi disciplinary working

- Roles and responsibilities

2

The Parent's View

'As parents we do not plan to have a child with ASD. Rather, we anticipate having children who, as they grow older, will themselves become self-sufficient and independent, and experience the desire to have their own children, in the same way that we have.'

Source : Attfield, E and Morgan, S.H. (2006) *Living with autistic spectrum disorders.* London: Paul Chapman/Sage Publications

3

Diagnosis and Parents

Carer Survey results

N = 614

Vast majority had concerns over child's development between ages of 12–36 months

(westmidlands. rcp.org.uk, 2001)

4

Diagnosis and Parents

Of which:

59 had concerns from 0–12 months

178 from 12–24 months

123 from 24–36 months

83 from 36–48 months

5

Diagnosis and Parents

Time gap between carer's concerns and receiving a diagnosis:

78 had a gap of 12 months
133 of 12–24 months
90 of 24–36 months
59 of 36–48 months
51 of 48–60 months

6

Diagnosis and Parents

And

40 waited

between

10 and 16 years

7

Diagnosis and Parents

63 percent were expecting a diagnosis of ASDs

but confirmation came as a

devastating blow.

8

The Parent's View

- Importance of understanding where parents are coming from

- The majority need more information on how to help their child

- And help for themselves to understand the condition

- The Internet plugs a gap but can be misleading

- You are an important link in this process

9

The Parent's View

- All parents want to know that they are doing the very best for their child

- Many parents have had to persist in getting any answers from professionals

- This can give them a "battling" mentality

- Which may lead to a false initial impression

- They need assurance that you are listening to their concerns and also have their child's best interests at heart

10

Legal Requirements upon Services

- The right to education

- The Disability Discrimination Acts

- Every Child Matters agenda

- SEN Code of Practice

- Special Educational Needs and Disability Act

11

The Right to Education

- It is important to remember that children with disabilities have not always had a right to education – 1970

- The trend towards inclusion in mainstream education is more than changing buildings

- Hearts and minds, attitudes and prejudices need engaging in the drive towards achieving inclusive schools

- 'The heart of inclusion is allowing for, and respecting, the right to be different'

Source: Plimley, L.A . and Bowen, M. (2006b) *Supporting Pupils with Autistic Spectrum disorders*. London: Paul Chapman/ Sage Publications.

12

Disability Discrimination Act (1995)

- Requires ALL educational establishments to make adaptations to their buildings/provision so that people with disabilities are not excluded

- ASDs are an 'invisible disability' but nevertheless require flexibility on the part of the service provider

- Physical access arrangements may require consideration for levels of tolerance and sensory difference, rather than ramps and lifts

Source : Department of Work and Pensions (1995) *The Disability Discrimination Act*. London: HMSO.

13

Disability Discrimination Act (1995)

- ALL schools need to make an annual report stating:

  – Arrangements for the admission of disabled pupils

  – Steps taken to prevent disabled pupils being treated less favourably than other pupils

  – Facilities provided to assist access to the school by disabled pupils

- The pupil with ASDs may provoke many creative challenges in fulfilling these requirements.

Source : Department of Work and Pensions (1995) *The Disability Discrimination Act*. London: HMSO.

14

Disability Discrimination Act (2005)

- Promotion of disability equality; encourage participation of disabled people in public life; eliminate unlawful discrimination

- Disability definition is different to SEN eligibility criteria

- Disability 'has a substantial and long term adverse effect on ability to carry out normal day to day activities' (DDA, 2005)

- Disability Equality scheme for every school – how the requirements will be met

Source: Department of Work and Pensions (2005) *The Disability Discrimination Act*. London: HMSO

15

Every Child Matters Agenda

- Be healthy

- Stay safe

- Enjoy and achieve

- Make a positive contribution

- Achieve economic well-being

Each of these aims requires whole staff debate on how to enable ALL pupils with disability to achieve

Source: Department for Education and Skills (2003) *Every Child Matters* www.everychildmatters.gov.uk

16

SEN Code of Practice (2001)

- Greater emphasis on parental involvement and pupil participation

- Introduction of the graduated response

- Offers practical advice on how to carry out duties to assess, identify and make provision for SEN

- Access to Parent Partnership services

Source: DfEs (2001) *The Code of Practice for Special Educational Needs.* Nottingham: DfES Publications.

17

SEN Code of Practice (2002)

- Greater emphasis on parental involvement and pupil participation – *how to ensure the wishes of parents and pupils are canvassed and acted upon*

- Introduction of the graduated response – *a flexible and responsive awareness of need*

- Offers practical advice on how to carry out duties to assess, identify and make provision for SEN – *many pupils with ASD cope well in their academic work but have additional needs in the social structures within school.*

- Access to Parent Partnership services – *making sure parents are aware of advice and support from PPS*

18

SENDA (2001)

- Disagreement resolution services
- Inclusion in all aspects of the pupil's school life
- Importance of risk assessment
- Accessibility strategy for each local authority
- Accessibility plans for each school
- Regular review of policies and protocols within schools to ensure those with disabilities are not unfavourably treated.

Source: Department of Education and Skills (DfES) (2001) *Special Educational Needs and Disability Act (SENDA).* London: HMSO.

19

Helpful Guidance for Professionals

- ASD Good Practice Guidance (DfES/DoH,2002)
- Quality Standards for ASD (WAG, 2007)
- Autistic Spectrum Disorders – a guide to classroom practice (DENI, 2003)
- ASD Teacher Toolkit (PAPA, DENI, 2003)
- 'Education for Pupils with Autism Spectrum Disorders' Report (HMIe, Scotland 2006)
- All Wales Strategic Action Plan for ASDs (WAG, 2007)
- The Northern Ireland Autism Act (in preparation)

Each of these initiatives will help agencies to plan their work together with parents

20

The Statutory Framework

- Graduated response (England, Wales)
- Co-ordinated support plans (Scotland)
  - A staged process which requires evidence based checks and balances at each stage
  - A flexible response to a continuum of need
  - Evidence needs to exist of plans, targets, differentiated work, involvement of SENCo in supporting the pupil
  - Involvement of specialist support services if child fails to make expected progress
- The school needs to keep parents informed at every stage

21

Working with in Partnership with Parents and Carers

- A true Open Door policy that lets parents know what is provided, when it is accessible and how to keep involved in the education of their child

- The involvement of parents in the identification of priorities, the setting of targets, the sharing of resources/strategies

- Learning from parents – professionals do not hold all the solutions

- Parents know their child best

22

Working with in Partnership with Parents and Carers continued

- Building blocks of effective partnerships
  - Mutual respect and tolerance
  - Belief in the experience, knowledge of each other
  - Willingness and commitment to work together
  - Honesty and realism
  - Positive communication, including listening
  - Cooperation and flexibility
  - Promotion of strengths
  - Accepting differences and moving on

Source: Attfield, E. and Morgan S. H. (2006) *Living with Autistic Spectrum Disorders.* London: Paul Chapman/Sage Publications.

23

Multi–Disciplinary Working

Other disciplines commonly involved:
- Paediatrician/diagnostician
- Psychologist – educational, clinical
- Speech and language/occupational/music/play therapy
- Local authority/children's services personnel
- Specialist/outreach support team
- Inspection services
- Local health trust personnel
- Child and Adult Mental Health service (CAMHS)
- Parent partnership service
- Careers/ Connexions
- Parents
- Schools
- AND other voluntary (charity) involvement

24

Multi–Disciplinary Working continued

- <u>Every Child Matters</u> Agenda is working towards more seamless services and support

- Schools can often be the cross over point where disciplines meet and discuss

- Opinions of disciplines can differ

- The common commitment must be towards the individual with ASD

- Parents find it helpful to have a small number of professionals to relate to

25

Multi–Disciplinary Working continued

- Collaboration is what is needed

- The setting up of joint Children's services will improve the blurring of professional boundaries

- Local area co-ordination groups can oversee the setting up of joint services and provide a focus on the needs of individuals with ASDs

- A 'champion' of ASD would be a key appointment to ensure that agencies worked together and kept parents informed

26

Roles and Responsibilities

- Everyone has a role to play from diagnosticians to local support groups

- Early identification and assessment is a key to giving parents a signpost to further support and services

- Co-ordinated support with schools, health, social services and the voluntary sector playing key roles – training and information will be vital

- Sharing of ideas and strategies will ensure continuity and consistency of approach to the individual

27

Improving Home School Links

- Endeavour to involve parents in the education pf their child
- Make invitations and 1:1 appointments to encourage their participation – once a year parents' evening will not suffice
- Make any information sent home as user friendly and jargon-free as possible
- Newsletters, home school diaries, video diaries, frequent texts or emails with good news will encourage parents to respond
- Use the telephone sparingly as it is often associated with emergencies
- Work towards achieving a 'Welcoming school' ethos

28

10

Planning for Transition

Individuals with ASDs do not like change and so it is important that any changes in circumstances are well planned in advance. This section gives an overview of the approaches that can be used to plan effectively for transition and recommends a number of strategies and ideas that can be used to assist in the process.

Planning

Given the difficulties many ASD pupils face in coping with change, it is important to place a strong emphasis on carefully planned transition across phases. The move from one provision to another therefore needs to be handled sensitively. Some local authorities now have designated officers with a responsibility for monitoring transition either across phases or within a phase.

A number of methods can be adopted in an attempt to ensure a smooth transition between pre-school services and mainstream school/special school/nursery/unit. At the pre-school phase – transition from pre-school to school – families and individuals with ASDs might be supported by professionals from health, education and social services giving transition planning a multi-agency focus.

In England and Wales, transition from primary to secondary education and from secondary phase to further education or employment tends to have an educational focus. Procedures outlined in the *Code of Practice* (DfES (2001)/ WAG (2002)) are used. Whether individuals with ASDs have a statement of special educational need or not, the LEA should give parents/carers and individuals with ASDs the opportunity to discuss appropriate schools to which they could apply. When individuals have a statement, the provision required in secondary school should be discussed at the Year 5 Annual Review.

There should be adequate record-keeping and profiling methods so that information should accompany the individuals with ASD as they move on. In this respect, Individual Education Plans (IEPs) must be up-to-date and annual reviews well documented. All pupils should have an individual file that details their strengths and difficulties. Ideally, an LEA officer with expertise in ASD should be available to support the school during the transition phase and develop partnerships with other schools who have the relevant expertise and experience. It is also advisable for schools to have a member of staff to link with the child to help them at times of transition, particularly in secondary schools where they have to relate to many different members of staff.

The transition from school to further education necessitates a partnership between the specialist career service and tertiary colleges. Where a pupil has attended a special school for many years or in some instances has been to a residential school, transition will need to be planned in advance using a phased/gradual move to the new service.

Preparation

With current educational trends moving towards more mainstream inclusion for children on the autistic spectrum (DfES, [2001], WAG, [2002], Audit Scotland/HMIe [2003]), the sooner the familiarization exercises start with the new environment and population, the better. Parents who have chosen mainstream primary schools for their youngsters with ASDs, can often feel unsettled when they are looking at secondary provision. Some might be concerned that the secondary environment is too large and too busy for their child and may even consider a special school placement. In some instances, local education authorities may have developed ASD resource bases attached to a designated mainstream school. If this is the case then transition planning between primary and secondary phases should be easier.

A greater emphasis on league tables and Standardized Assessment Tasks (SATs), might mean that larger primary schools may be moving towards a similar model of provision and support as secondary schools. However, the proximity difference between the two environments may not suit the child with ASDs. The primary stage is characterized by *local* provision, i.e. most primary schools are located within the child's community, parents know staff and vice versa. A secondary school may be at a distance from home and only accessible on school transport. The lack of personal contact and the efficient ethos of secondary schools, with a high emphasis on conformity, may mean that mainstream in Year 7 is a very difficult option for parents and carers to accept.

However, with careful planning many obstacles can be overcome. For example, more inclusive secondary schools are taking greater responsibility when it comes to easing the transition of pupils with disabilities by early and effective exercises to support their future learners. Secondary School Special Educational Needs Co-ordinators (SENCos) are advised to keep in contact with their primary counterparts in order to identify pupils in need of support as early as Year 4 or 5. This may make all the difference to transition across phases being a success.

Sometimes, support contracts are issued and attached to a certain number of hours for a named child within a particular setting; sadly this may end once the child moves to a new setting. Often a new member of support staff will be appointed with a different contract. Although this is understandable, it can be another change that the child has to learn to accept and therefore needs careful consideration in transition planning.

Plimley and Bowen (2006a: 2) suggest the following when planning for transition:

- Procedures outlined in *The SEN Code of Practice* (WAG, 2002/DfES, 2001) should be noted.
- The views, feelings and anxieties of the child with ASDs should be considered at all times.
- Secondary and Primary SENCos should have regular dialogue throughout the school year.
- Secondary SENCos should attend annual reviews of children with a Statement of Special Need in Year 5 and Year 6.
- Child with an ASD visits the Secondary school as often as possible in the summer term, prior to the Open Day when all potential Year 7 students attend.
- Nominated member of Secondary staff gives pastoral support to the child early on.
- There should be adequate record-keeping and profiling methods so that all relevant information can accompany individuals with ASDs as they move on.
- Parents of a child with ASDs are invited into Secondary school to talk about their child's differences.
- Staff make up an Action Plan around the support needs of the child.
- Sensory and environmental adjustments are pre-empted and accommodated.
- The Secondary environment is labelled and made more visually clear.
- The Secondary environment is made into a CD-ROM 'virtual map' as a guide for ALL new pupils (Cook and Stowe, 2003) well in advance of their start date.
- All Secondary staff have an awareness-raising session using case studies of pupils with ASDs who they know.
- The Secondary environment has a breaktime 'safe haven' room available for all vulnerable pupils.
- The Secondary SENCo has a portable file of accessible information on all conditions present in the pupil population of the school.
- The Secondary SENCo has quick checklists for each teacher containing guidance on how to teach pupils with different conditions.
- There is a peer buddy system in place.
- There is a 'Circle of Friends' (Whitaker, Barratt, Joy, Potter and Thomas, 1998) mechanism within school.
- All channels for communication are kept open.

Useful resources

Broderick, K. and Mason-Williams, T. (eds) (2005) *Transition Toolkit,* Kidderminster. British Institute of Learning Disabilities (BILD). This toolkit contains some very practical exercises for use by schools and key personnel. Templates of useful transition documents contain valid information for key people help to ensure that details are documented in one place. The book also contains photocopiable resources and encourages full and appropriate participation of the child/young person.

Kirby, A. and Drew, S. (2001) *Transition. Development Co-ordination Disorder (DCD)/Dyspraxia Practical Resource book for secondary to further education and employment.* Cardiff: The Dyscovery Centre. Visit www.dyscovery.co.uk. This book contains some useful checklists and photocopiable resources for student use. Although aimed at students with DCD, yet many of the strategies suggested could be successfully used with individuals with an ASD.

Sholl, C., Dancyger, F., Parsons, M. and Dale, C. (2006) *Transition Pathways: Guidance and Tools to Support Person-centred Transition Planning with Young Disabled People aged 13–25.* Visit http://www.solihull.gov.uk/upload/public/attachments/24/TransitionPathwayp1.pdf. This resource covers students moving on from school to further education, employment, training, residential college and daytime activities. The materials enable agencies to understand the process from the young person's point of view. This book is well presented and contains practical ideas for schools to use.

 Case studies

Use the information and suggestions given in the presentation to create a transition plan for the following individuals with an ASD. Think carefully about who will need to be involved in the process and appropriate timescales and strategies based on individual needs.

Early Years – Katie aged 4

Katie has been attending a local pre-school playgroup with support for three mornings a week. In six months' time, she is due to attend a local primary school with a specialist resource base for Key Stage 1 children with ASDs. She will travel by taxi to school. Katie uses picture symbols to communicate her needs.

Primary – Rory aged 11

Rory attends a local primary school and has some part-time support. In September, he moves to a secondary school that is four miles away from his home. At the moment, Rory's mother or grandmother walks with him to school. Rory does not respond well to sudden loud noises such as buzzers or bells. At playtime, he is allowed to return to the classroom just before the bell rings. He also finds lunchtimes difficult, especially determining what he wants to eat. Rory's special interests are chess and computers.

Young Adult – Ali aged 15

Since the age of fourteen, Ali has had a transition plan and has been consulted continuously about what he wants to do post school. After a very successful work experience placement at a garden centre, Ali has decided that he would like to go to the horticultural college in the next town. The manager of the garden centre where he did his work experience placement has offered him a Saturday job.

 Extension activities

These activities can be used with a range of people – teaching assistants; teachers, whole school staff; and parents – to provoke discussion. We would recommend that you use the appropriate case study with the matching extension activity whenever possible, e.g. Rory's case study with the first extension activity. These extension activities give participants the opportunity to reflect upon what they have learnt in the lecture and consider some genuine practical solutions to problems.

- Ask participants to get into small groups of four or five. Ask them to make a list of the positive features of being in a primary school for individuals with ASDs. Then ask them

Continued

to think about the secondary school and how it will differ. Ask the group to come up with some strategies that might help the individual with ASDs to cope with some of the major differences between the environments.

- Ask participants to get into groups and consider an individual with ASDs who is about to leave school for further education. Ask them to make a list of all the people that will be needed to be involved. If participants are from the same local area, ask them to list the names and contact details of any professionals they have noted.
- Give each group of participants a Transition Plan to discuss. Does it meet the core areas related to further education, health, housing, transport, work, relationships and hobbies? Give them the list of questions relating to the young person, the family, the school and the professionals from the section on Transition Planning in the *SEN Toolkit* (DfES, 2002). Does the Plan address all the issues?

Recommended reading

In this section we recommend books that address issues outlined in government documents in addition to guidance from professionals, the voluntary sector and individuals with ASDs.

DfES (2002) *Section 10: Transition Planning. The SEN Toolkit.* Available to download on www.teachernet.gov.uk. This information booklet which was published as part of the SEN Toolkit offers some useful and comprehensive advice to the reader based on issues relating to the Code of Practice.

Plimley, L.A. and Bowen, M. (2006) *ASDs in the Secondary School,* London:Paul Chapman/Sage Publications. This book has chapters on the move from primary to secondary, preparation for employment and accreditation and examination, all of which will inform thinking on issues relating to transition planning.

Salter, K. and Twidle, R. (2005) *The Learning Mentor's Source and Resource Book,* Chapter 9. Trowbridge: Lucky Duck and PCP. This excellent book provides the reader a number of strategies and activities that can be used to make transition easier. The chapter also contains work sheets which can be accessed using the accompanying CD-Rom.

Segar, M. (1997) *Coping:Survival Guide for People with Asperger Syndrome,* www.autismandcomputing. org.uk/marc2.htm Mark Segar's work is a first-hand account covering a range of issues but giving some useful hints and tips on interview skills and the move from education to employment.

SEN Partnership (S.E. Region), Surrey County Council and National Autistic Society (2005) *Breaking Down Barriers to Learning: Practical Strategies for Achieving Successful Transition for Students with Autism and Asperger Syndrome.* Available from www.nas.org.uk. A useful booklet that looks at the transition planning from school into further/higher education and employment.

Welsh Assembly Government (WAG) (2007) *Policy Review of Additional Educational Needs. Part 3: Transition.* Cardiff: National Assembly for Wales. Welsh Assembly Government review on Transition highlights best practice in this area. It is useful to use as a set of standards or goals in transition planning.

Useful websites

www.connexions.gov.uk
www.dfes.gov.uk
www.wales.gov.uk
www.enquire.org.uk
www.lsc.gov.uk
www.careerswales.com
www.careers-scotland.org
www.skill.org.uk
www.jobcentreplus.gov.uk
www.afse.org.uk
www.remploy.co.uk
www.nas.org.uk
www.awares.org

 Go to the accompanying CD-Rom for the full selection of slides that accompany this section and remember you can also access detailed speaker notes to use with each slide.

Section 10:

PLANNING FOR TRANSITION

1

Transition Planning

'I was sensitive to change. I was terrified of it, because change leapt into the unknown and I could not get my head around exactly what the unknown was ... I had to exert my control by building a definite routine out of school life'.

Source: Jackson, N. (2002) *Standing Down Falling Up, Asperger Syndrome from the Inside Out*, Bristol: Lucky Duck Publishing.

2

The Early Years

- Could involve move from settings provided by health, social services or the voluntary sector into a mainstream or special school environment

- Separation process from familiar adults such as parents and carers needs careful forward planning

- It is important to consider continuity

3

Useful Meetings (PAPA,2003)

- Meeting of a range of people such as parents, SENCo, Teaching Assistants, health professionals, pre-school setting staff and the Head Teacher

- Meeting of school staff to consider outcome of the multi-agency meeting and draw up an IEP and transition plan

- Meetings between parents and school staff

4

Points to Consider (Bache et al., 2004)

- What strategies and language is the child familiar with at home?
- Would this be appropriate in the new setting?
- Does the child have particular sensitivities such as food, touch, smell sleep?
- How did the child settle into other settings?
- Were any particular strategies used that could support the move?

Source: Bache, K. et al. (2004) *Guidelines for Working with Children with ASDs at Foundation Phase of KS1*, www.southglos.gov.uk

5

Transition from Primary to Secondary

- Should start in Year 5 and be part of the IEP

- Phasing out support and developing independence where necessary

- Meetings between parents, individual with ASDs, relevant staff from both schools to consider any potential difficulties in Year 6

6

Transition from Primary to Secondary School continued

- Arrange series of transition/familiarization visits incorporating classroom time and also break and lunch times

- Make a booklet or DVD of the new school environment and the staff

- Consider support mechanisms for move from one lesson to another—colour coding books to subjects and rooms

7

In the Secondary School ...

- How can the timetable be explained?
- Can individual with ASDs have designated seating in classrooms?
- Do the peer group need educating and would a buddy system be useful?
- How much adult support will be required especially in the early days?
- Are there toileting issues?

8

Other Strategies
(Cook and Stowe, 2003)

- A sound transition plan
- Devising a pupil passport
- Playing board games to rehearse the transition
- Colour coding of timetables and exercise books
- Work Shadowing

Source: Cook, L.L and Stowe, S. (2003) Talk given on Nottingham Inclusion Support Service at Distance Education (ASD) weekend, School of Education, University of Birmingham.

Transition Plan 14+

- A Transition Plan must be drawn up for individuals with a statement of SEN in Year 9
- It should address core areas, such as FE, employment, health, housing, transport, relationships and hobbies
- The TP may change and grow over time

Underlying Principles
(DfES SEN Toolkit, 2002)

- Participative
- Holistic
- Supportive
- Evolving
- Inclusive
- Colloborative

Source: Department for Education and Skills (2002) SEN Toolkit. www.dfes.gov.uk/sen

Who is Involved?

- The young person
- The family
- The School
- A range of professionals dependent on future needs-including social services and careers advisers, e.g. Careers Wales, Connexions

Points to Consider for Individuals with ASDs

- Are plans in place well in advance for familiarization visits at different times of the day?
- How much student support (FE) or mentor support (work) will be required?
- Are the plans realistic and achievable?
- Is there any way in which special interests can be incorporated into employment opportunities or any area of study?

Points to Consider for Individuals with ASDs continued

- Are there any sensory issues that will need to be addressed in the new environment?
- Are their opportunities within the setting to teach the hidden social rules, health and safety rules, and general rules?
- Is there somewhere that the individual can 'escape' when stress levels reach an all time high?
- Are arrangements in place for lunch-times and break-times?

Finally..

Whether the transition is from one institution to another or from one activity to another always find time to discuss any genuine concerns individuals with ASDs and their family might have. Be sensitive to these concerns, however minor they might appear on the surface

11

Intervention Programmes – TEACCH, PECS and Social Stories

> ☀ This section considers how to navigate the vast amount of information there is now available to parents and professionals on effective approaches to supporting those individuals with ASDs, and looks in detail at three of the most widely used approaches.

Professionals and parents face an overwhelming amount of information when looking for effective approaches for children with ASDs. Parents in particular can be very vulnerable to information contained in articles in the media, claiming the latest cure or therapeutic intervention. Teachers too will often come across information via professional media and on training courses. They also experience parents who visit school with information maybe downloaded from the Internet and a strong wish for the staff's professional opinion. A current Google search for the words intervention and autism yields 1.15 million potential references for an interested seeker of further details.

Many parents and professionals are seeking impartial help to find something that works for their child and the plethora of available information via, such mechanisms as Google, can lead to many false starts and blind alleys. Parents are especially vulnerable to heavily marketed approaches that can claim to 'cure' or 'bring the child out of their autism.' Parents of a child with a condition with no known cure could be susceptible to this sort of commercialism. Professionals can help parents to refine their search and draw upon recognized critiques of interventions and approaches, such as Research Report 77 – Educational interventions for children with autism (Jordan, Jones and Murray, 1998) and more internationally, Dawson and Osterling (1997). Both pieces of research underline that one of the most successful elements in any approach or intervention is that it can be given a continuity of application between home and school. Where parents are key to the implementation of the intervention, then the best possible conditions for its success are ensured.

Dawson and Osterling (1997) also say that the most effective intervention programmes have the following characteristics:

- A focus on specific skills that are to be learned.
- The structure of the environment enables the opportunity for skills and knowledge to be transferred (generalization).
- The components of the programme give predictability and routine.
- The intervention involves the whole family.

With these features in mind we now look at three of the popular and current approaches on offer to parents and professionals in the UK. Each shares the continuity of resources and instruction between home and school.

1   **TEACCH – T**reatment and **E**ducation of **A**utistic and **C**ommunication handicapped **CH**ildren (Schopler and Mesibov, 1995). The TEACCH approach focuses on the individual's strengths and emerging skills. It taps into typical features of ASDs to provide security and familiarity

in work and other routines, gives predictability, structure and can be tailored to the learning needs of the individual. Many structures are conveyed using visual or graphical information so that a permanent system of reference can be presented in a logical order. Schopler and Mesibov claim that TEACCH strategies can be used from 'cradle to grave' to support the individual through their lives.

2   **PECS – P**icture **E**xchange **C**ommunication **S**ystem (Bondy and Frost, 1994). The PECS programme works to give the individual with ASDs a functional form of communication. The programme uses symbols to convey information in grammatical format. Introduction of the programme focuses on what motivates and reinforces the individual and initial approaches gain attention and cooperation by using motivators to engage the interest of the individual. The PECS approach rests on the need for the individual to recognize that effective, functional communication of any sort relies on there being an initiator of communication, a recipient to communicate with and a topic/object to communicate about. Once the individual learns that they have to communicate to another about something, then a vocabulary of symbols, sentences and the spoken word quickly builds up.

3   **Social Stories** (Gray, 1994, 2000). Social stories work to assist the individual to understand the social rules and expectations of everyday situations that they may find problematic. A situation that an individual cannot understand, tolerate or respond appropriately to, is presented in a personalized story to the individual. The story will explain what is happening socially in the situation, giving the perspectives of others, some social information and some guidelines on how to manage the situation better. By keeping the individual at the centre of the story, the load on comprehension is made lighter because the story deals in explicit details. Again, the approach keeps a permanent record for the individual to refer to again and again.

Useful resources

Writing with symbols – http://www.widgit.com/products/wws2000/index.htm
Elkan training materials for further ideas on how to introduce Social Stories and Comic Strip conversations, available from Elklan, 156, High Street, Holywood, County Down, NI.

Gray, A.C. (2000) *New Social Story Book Illustrated Edition.* Arlington, TX: Future Horizons.
Gray, A.C. and Leigh White, A. (eds) (2002) *My Social Stories Book.* Arlington, TX: Future Horizons.
Both Carol Gray titles give plenty of examples and ideas for using Social Story strategies to personalize social messages.
Schopler, E. and Mesibov, G. (1995) 'Structured teaching in the TEACCH approach,' in E. Schopler and G. Mesibov (eds), *Learning and Cognition in Autism.* New York: Plenum Press.

 Case studies

Early Years – Marvin aged 3

Marvin has been at the provision for three weeks now and no-one has heard him use any words at all. His mother says that he will use simple one-word responses occasionally at home, most often 'No' He gets frustrated when no-one can interpret what he wants in free-choice time. He enjoys stories and rhymes but does not join in with repetitive details/rhymes.

What approach, from TEACCH, PECs or Social Stories covered in this Section, would you choose as an initial strategy to tackle this situation ?

Primary – Sasha aged 8

Sasha keeps up with academic work in the Juniors and has a gift for mental arithmetic in particular. What she seems to lack though are self-and work-organization skills. She is expected to assemble the books and equipment she needs in some subjects and bring PE and swimming kit from home. She seems perpetually bemused when these expectations arise and she gets very stressed out by not knowing what she needs and the order in which to proceed. It has been known for her father to have to come into school during the day to bring in vital, forgotten equipment.

Continued

What approach, from TEACCH, PECs or Social Stories covered in this Section, would you choose as an initial strategy to tackle this situation ?

Secondary – Julian aged 14

Julian is coping very well with his Secondary curriculum but is lacking in age-appropriate social skills. He is at the difficult age where adolescents want to be in with a crowd but his attempts to impress peers are infantile and he is further ostracized by them. While his male classmates are focusing their socialization efforts on attracting female admiration, Julian has picked up some comic catchphrases from a popular TV series and makes remarks that could verge on insult rather than positively attracting a girl's attention.

What approach, from TEACCH, PECs or Social Stories covered in this Section, would you choose as an initial strategy to tackle this situation ?

Special – Parvinder aged 17

Parvinder is using the vocational curriculum to develop some gainful leisure and employment skills. He has a particular interest in helping in the school's greenhouses where plants are propagated for sale at school and in the local community. Whilst he is good at tending healthy plants, despite being shown how to transplant and pot on cuttings several times, he does not seem to have remembered how to work through the process.

What approach, from TEACCH, PECs or Social Stories covered in this Section, would you choose as an initial strategy to tackle this situation ?

Residential – Chung aged 11

Chung is well-adjusted to the demands of the school curriculum but often has flashpoints during the times before and after school in his residential house. He has responded well to the use of a structured approach to working through personal hygiene and dressing and washing skills but he has difficulty in initiating conversation and expressing his own wishes. He does have an extensive, if idiosyncratic, vocabulary but he does not use it in situations when he has a strong desire to get something or do something. He will just go and do it. This has led to Health and Safety issues over him pulling equipment down from shelves or running off to explore the school grounds.

What approach, from TEACCH, PECs or Social Stories covered in this Section, would you choose as an initial strategy to tackle this situation ?

Young adult – Lauren aged 20

Lauren is living in a small supported housing scheme with two others who have Asperger syndrome. Lauren has a reasonable level of independence and can use the local community resources for shopping, travelling to different places and leisure activities. Lauren has many age-appropriate skills and behaviours but one thing is really annoying her peers and the staff at the scheme – her love of using the full-length mirror in the hall to preen and pamper herself each time she passes it. She can spend nearly half-an-hour in front of the mirror on occasions and while this does not cause too much of a problem when people are out of in their rooms, it can lead to heavy congestion during busy times. Lauren has a smaller mirror in her room but she prefers to use the full-length one.

What approach, from TEACCH, PECs or Social Stories covered in this Section, would you choose as an initial strategy to tackle this situation ?

 ## Extension activities

The following suggested extension activities will help a provision to build up resources and strategies from the three programmes and to introduce and develop each programme according to individual needs.

- Build up resources and ideas from these three approaches to give a consistency of use.
- Keep a dialogue with others to develop and progress your ideas.

Continued

- Use a problem-solving approach, similar to the ideas in the Case Studies, using the details of individuals known to you.
- Action plan the introduction of one of these approaches to target a particular issue.
- Define some common elements from the approaches that could be adopted with consistency in your setting.
- Prioritize the changes needed (staffing/environment) in order to introduce one of these approaches.
- How can you involve home and family in applying the principles of one of these approach to ensure the maximum continuity of strategy ?
- In small groups/teams departments write a social story about a common school issue – Child A will not relinquish his place at the head of the line at the end of break. This causes conflict and upset with others and makes a poor start to the next session.
- In small groups/teams departments write a TEACCH timetable for Child B who always turns up to lessons late and constantly gets lost around the school buildings.
- In small groups/teams departments write a strategy for introducing PECs for a child who does not appreciate that he needs to have a communicative partner (i.e. someone to talk to) as he is constantly having a dialogue with inanimate objects.

Recommended reading

The following texts give further background to each of the programmes in this section.

Bondy, L. and Frost, L. (1994) The Delaware autistic programme, in S.L. Harris and J.S. Handleman (eds), *Preschool Education Programs for Children with Autism.* Austin, TX: Pro-ed.

Gray, A.C. (1994) *The Social Story Book.* Arlington, TX: Future Horizons.

Schopler, E. and Mesibov, G. (1995) Structured teaching in the TEACCH approach, in E. Schopler and G. Mesibov (eds), *Learning and Cognition in Autism.* New York: Plenum Press.

Useful websites

The Picture Exchange Communication System PECS USA – http://www.pecs.com/WhatsPECS.htm

PECS UK sources:

http://www.pecs.org.uk – Pyramid education consultants training details
http://www.pecs.org.uk/shop/asp/default.asp/ for ordering resources
http://callcentre.education.ed.ac.uk/ – PECS in Scotland
PECs training information – http://www.fastuk.org/services/courseview.php?id=54

Social Stories

Society for the Autistically Handicapped (SFTAH) Northamptonshire training venue for Social Story training– http://www.autismuk.com/index4asub2.htm
Carol Gray Center for Social Stories – http://www.thegraycenter.org/socialstories.cfm
Contact Carol Gray to ask questions about social skills – http://autism.about.com/b/a/257546.htm

TEACCH

Society for the Autistically Handicapped (SFTAH) Northamptonshire training venue for TEACCH – http://www.autismuk.com/index4asub1.htm
Sunfield School, Worcestershire, programme for TEACCH training – http://www.sunfield.org.uk/courses.htm
Autism Cymru training programme for TEACCH training – www.awares.org
The UK Training Index for training courses in TEACCH – http://www.underoak.co.uk/public-courses/medical_training/learning_disabilities.htm
Visual communication Ispeek freebie resources – www.ispeek.co.uk.
Visual timetable cards – www.tes.co.uk/resources/Resources.aspx?resourceId=2174

An overview of websites for other approaches

EARLYBIRD   www.nas.org.uk and key word search EarlyBird
GREENSPAN   www.coping.org/earlyin/floortm.htm
HANEN   www.hanen.org
INTENSIVE INTERACTION   www.intensiveinteraction.co.uk
LOVAAS   www.lovaas.com
NAS   www.nas.org.uk
OPTION   www.option.org
PORTAGE   www.portage.org.uk
SPELL   www.nas.org.uk and keyword search SPELL

 Go to the accompanying CD-Rom for the full selection of slides that accompany this section and remember you can also access detailed speaker notes to use with each slide.

Section 11:

INTERVENTION PROGRAMMES – TEACCH, PECS AND SOCIAL STORIES

1

Current Approaches

- TEACCH

- PECS

- Social Stories

2

Current Approaches

THINGS TO BE BORNE IN MIND ...

- Does this approach address all 3 impairments?

- What do the adults and children do in this approach?

- What is the rationale for this approach?

3

THINGS TO BE BORNE IN MIND ...

(continued)

- What are the approach's expected outcomes?

- What evidence is there to suggest that these outcomes can be achieved?

4

TEACCH

(**T**reatment and **E**ducation of **A**utistic and **C**ommunications handicapped **CH**ildren)

- Offers a cradle–to–grave approach
- Assesses strengths and emerging skills
- Teaches structure and routine
- Importance of Visual clarity
- Work, then favoured activity

Source: Schopler, E. and Mesibov, G. (1995) Structured teaching in the TEACCH approach, in E.Schopler, and G. Mesibov, (eds), *Learning and Cognition in Autism.* New York: PlenumPress.

5

TEACCH continued

- Adaptable to whatever situation

- Supports parents in process

- Provides the answer to 4 most urgent questions

- What are we doing, how much, when finished, what next ?

6

TEACCH Visual Structures

- A Schedule
- A Jig
- A Timetable
- A Time line
- A countdown to …..
- An Organizer
- A Filofax

7

1	Go to your place
2	Sit on your chair
3	Take your first work tray on the left
4	Get out the stacking cups
5	With the largest first, make a stack of 7 cups
6	Show your stack to Mrs Begum

8

TEACCH Systems

- Left to right
- Top to bottom
- First one first
- Then take off/cross off/put away
- Work baskets/finish baskets
- Transition areas
- No visual distracters
- Functional skills

9

TEACCH Works Well to Teach

- Times of the day and events
- Dressing order
- Tasks and activities
- Self-care skills - hair care, teeth, bathing, personal hygiene
- Community–based skills, e.g. car washing, gardening, decorating, shopping, some employment opportunities that are routine–based

10

Secondary TEACCH Timetable for a Morning

- Registration
- Lesson 1 – History, go to room 15, Mrs Harding
- Lesson 2 – English, go to room 22 on second floor, Mr Davies – Miss Smith is on a course today
- Break time – Year 8 pupils are doing a playground survey, collect your clipboard from Ms Taylor (form tutor) and join Alison and Paul to start survey

Remember to get a drink from the water dispenser

- Lesson 3 – French, go to French lab on first floor, Melle Bouchand
- Lesson 4 – Science, go to Science lab on <u>first</u> floor, not the second floor today, Mr Tudor

11

Primary TEACCH Timetable for a Morning

- Registration
- Literacy Hour
  - Whole class task
  - Group task, join with Paul, Alison and Peter as usual
  - Individual task, get out your exercise book
  REMEMBER – Draw a line under the last piece of work, put today's date and a title
  - Then complete 6 questions
- <u>Break time, don't forget to get a drink from the water dispenser. Mrs Jones has a job for you to do in the playground today</u>

12

Primary Morning continued

- Numeracy Hour
  — Whole class mental arithmetic task
  — Group task, join with Joshua, Harriet and Leah to measure your set of articles.
  — Individual task, complete 3 pages in your Maths text book.
- COMPUTER TIME! 10 minutes only – Remember to set timer and leave when it rings.
- Classroom jobs–ask Mrs Jones what needs doing today.

13

TEACCH and the Triad

- TEACCH can be adapted to address
  - Social Interaction, by enabling social skills to be practised using TEACCH structures and prompts
  - Communication, by using a structured approach to learning a communication system
  - Flexibility of thought and behaviour by using the structure to introduce new ideas, changes to routines, unknown information (e.g. possible room changes)

14

PECS

(**P**icture **E**xchange **C**ommunication **S**ystem)

- Visual system of teaching communication
- Uses object cards to express desires
- Bases first steps on person's interests
- Needs at least 2 adults
- 1 prompts person to ask for object
- Adult 2 prompts person to use card displaying object.

Source: Bondy, A and Frost, L. (1994) 'The Delaware autistic program', in S.L. Harris and J.S. Handleman (eds), *Preschool Education Programs for Children with Autism.* Austin, Texas: Pro-Ed.

15

PECS continued

- Person picks up card for crisps (already assessed as a favourite food)
- Gives to adult 1, who models 'Oh Sam wants crisps'
- Once person gets used to card exchange, then grammar and extended sentences are used
- Symbol/words cards I want …. To teach requests

16

PECS continued

- Moves onto 'I can see…'/'I can smell…'/'I am doing….'/
  …….. To develop reciprocal communication

- Sentence strips on Velcro build into a personal communication book that they can carry around with them

- High rate of success in teaching spoken communication

17

PECS and the Triad

- PECS can be adapted to address

  – Social Interaction, by teaching that communication needs a person, a topic and another person to 'hear' about the topic

  – Communication, it gives a clear and easy means of communicating with or without language

  – Flexibility of thought and behaviour, by using PECs symbols, situations can be negotiated and information shared

18

Social Stories

- A Social story is
  – a short story
  – written in a specific style
  – following a specific format
  – a description of a specified social situation
  – outlines what is happening socially
  – what people do
  – why they do it
  – what are the common responses
  – what are the expectations
- The goal is
  'To teach social understanding over rote compliance, to describe more than direct …'

Source: Gray, A.C. (1994) *Social Stories*. Arlington, TX: Future Horizons

19

The Purpose of a Social Story

- To give the child positive feedback – affirm their current skills and understanding

- To help shape a response to something more acceptable

- To aid their tolerance of a circumstance

- To help to anticipate or prepare for something new

- To stem a severe over–reaction which arises from a lack of understanding

20

How Social Stories Fit with Recognized Strategies for People with ASDs

- Liking for familiar
- Need to have individualisation
- Visual clarity
- Something to refer to
- Transitions need planning
- Need positive reinforcement
- Information needs to be pared to essentials

- *In a familiar format*
- *Each story is about them, tailored to them*
- *Written /symbolic*
- *Permanent record*
- *Changes are dealt with*
- *Stories affirm where they are at*
- *Vital factual information is there*

21

Devising a Social Story

- Sentence types -
  – Descriptive - truth, factual, assumption-free
    - 'My name is ……..; sometimes my dad reads to me'
  – Perspective – describe your internal knowledge, thoughts, opinions, feelings, beliefs, health
    - 'Some children like to finish their work before lunch; my sister believes in Father Christmas'
  – Directive – identifies a suggested response or a gentle prompt about behaviour
    - 'I will try and stay in my chair; I will pour my own drink'
  – Affirmative – enhance meaning and share a group value
    - 'Most people wash their hands after going to the toilets'

22

- Other sentence types
  – Control - written by the individual as a personal reference for them
    - 'When my teacher says this I know I must do that …'
  – Co-operative sentences - identifies what others will do to assist the person
    - 'My mom, dad and teacher will help me to …'
- THE RECIPE (Rowe,1999)
- For a 10 sentence story, the suggested ratio is
  - 1 directive sentence
  - 2-5 each of descriptive and perspective sentences

Source: Rowe, C. (1999). Do Social Stories benefit children with autism in mainstream primary school? *British Journal of Special Education*, 26 (1), 12-14.

23

A Good Example

How to walk with Mum

- When we go out to shops, Mum takes me in the car
- She parks the car in the car park by Tesco
- Mum likes me to hold her hand when we walk
- She says that will keep me safe
- She likes me to hold her hand when we get out of the car and walk over to the shopping centre
- When we get the shops I can walk by her side
- That will keep me safe
- I will try to hold her hand when we get out of the car and go to the shopping centre

24

Popular Uses for Social Stories

- Washing hands
- Blowing your nose
- Taking a nap
- Bedtime and sleeping
- Unexpected noises
- Babysitters
- Eating out
- Learning to shake someone's hand
- Thermometers
- Setting the table
- Homework
- Supply teachers

25

Social Stories and the Triad

- Social stories can be adapted to address

  - Social Interaction, to address how to behave appropriately in social situations; give insight into what others expect

  - Communication, to develop dialogue skills and understand humour and idioms

  - Flexibility of thought and behaviour, to move towards adapting inappropriate responses but focusing on what others (NTs) do in the same situation

26

12

Carrying Out a School Audit and Planning for Access and Inclusion

> This section gives an overview of the value of self-evaluation tools in improving the quality of provision and in the formulation of short-, medium-and long-term plans for pupils with ASDs. A number of published and unpublished audits now exist. This section also focuses on some of the issues that such tools might address, e.g. policy and procedure for ASDs, identification and assessment, environment. Also included in this section is an overview of the Disability Equality Duty and School Access Plans, which also impact on service provision for children and young people with ASDs.
>
> This section has a slightly different format from the others. The PowerPoint slides included in this section are intended for use as part of the training activity to highlight issues to consider for pupils with ASDs in relation to Self-Evaluation, School Access and Inclusion Plans and the Disability Equality Duty. The facilitator may choose to include other points from the text depending on the audience.

Improving provision for pupils with ASDs through self-evaluation

Ofsted and the DfES(2005: 4) argue that there are four key points about self-evaluation that schools should keep in mind:

- Rigorous self-evaluation helps schools to improve; it should not be undertaken solely for the purpose of inspection.
- Schools should shape for themselves a process that is simple and integrated within their routine management systems.
- Schools must listen to and do something about the views of their stakeholders.
- The school's recorded summary of its self-evaluation process should be updated at least annually and include information about the impact of its action on learners; assertions; and lists of initiatives that are unhelpful.

Ofsted and the DfES state that thorough self-evaluation provides the best means to identify strengths and weaknesses; from these, arise the key priorities for improvement. They go on to say that self-evaluation is only effective if it is based on openness, honesty and trust. Evidence gathered from self-evaluation should be analyzed and used fully to:

- Diagnose precisely where strengths and weaknesses lie and the implications for change.
- Identify the key priorities.
- Plan the action needed to bring about improvement.

As part of Autism Cymru's 'Inclusive Schools and ASDs: Whole School Training Project,' a number of schools across Wales have used a Self-Evaluation Tool to monitor their provision for pupils with ASDs. They have all been encouraged to be open and honest and to recognize that each will be in a very different position dependent upon their experiences of having pupils with ASDs in the school.

Schools can use published tools, such as those developed by DfES (2002) or create their own. If they choose the latter, it is important that schools make sure that a number of pertinent issues are addressed. They might also like to consider where the evidence exists. For example, the school may not have a discrete policy for ASDs but may have reference to ASDs in their School Access and Inclusion Plan, Behaviour Management Policy, Health and Safety Policy and Curriculum Policy. If this is the case, then it should be noted.

The action plan resulting from the audit should address issues where there is currently no evidence. Actions undertaken need to be realistic and any evidence put forward should clearly relate to the standard or objective set. Getting other staff on board will not be an easy task so it is important that one or two members of staff lead the way in raising awareness of the issues and assuring staff that ultimately the process will help them, rather than add to their workload. Time will also need to be set aside for the staff to discuss the self-evaluation tool and contribute to the proposed action plan.

Figure 12.1 available on the CD-Rom is a checklist of issues that schools will need to consider.

Clearly, schools will need to prioritize and tackle issues in bite-size pieces. Here are some examples of short term targets set by schools following self-evaluation:

School 1 is a small school for children aged between four and seven years. The school has two children in Nursery Class who are undergoing assessment for a diagnosis of ASDs. The nursery age (four to five years) children have a large open-plan classroom which can often become very busy when children are engaged in a mixture of activities. At lunch and breaktimes, the playground can also be over-stimulating. The school has a small staff and so communication is manageable. Staff meetings are held on a weekly basis. Priorities for School 1 included the following:

- Continue to modify the general school environment to take account of sensory issues.
- Staff will share information on ASDs in a formal way when they return from a training event.
- There will be an up-to-date bank of resources for ASDs.
- The school will develop a specific policy for pupils with ASDs.

School 2 is a large junior school and caters for pupils aged between seven and eleven years. The school has three pupils with ASDs in different classes throughout the school. Two of these pupils have help from a support worker. The head teacher of the school is committed to making the school more ASD-friendly but realizes that this needs to be done one step at a time. School staff have watched one pupil with ASDs grow in independence and would like to see the other two pupils with ASDs become less reliant on their support workers. They are also aware that, for two of the children, stress levels are at an all-time high during lunch and breaktimes. Priorities in this school therefore include:

- A policy on ASDs will be developed and written in conjunction with outside agencies and the voluntary sector.
- Pupils with ASDs will be more involved in decision making.
- Time will be given to pupils with ASDs to follow a special interest.
- A section of the library will be used as a 'safe haven' when pupils with ASDs are experiencing 'meltdown'.

These aspects are to be prioritized for attention in the School Development Plan.

School 3 is a secondary school for pupils aged between eleven and sixteen years. The school has recently admitted three pupils with a diagnosis of ASDs and as knowledge and understanding of the spectrum increases amongst staff, teachers are aware that they may also have other pupils with similar difficulties, despite their lack of a formal diagnosis. Three members of the school staff attended a two-day workshop and returned to school to carry out an audit and examine priorities. They certainly felt that with a new cohort of pupils with ASDs starting at the school they needed to carry out a review of existing policies and consider ways in which they can raise awareness across the whole school. They were also sensitive to the fact that the new pupils could have an adverse reaction to their new environment. This school therefore set itself the following priorities across the academic year:

- To develop a policy document in consultation with outside agencies
- To have a whole school training day on ASDs
- To create a resource bank of materials in the staffroom
- To put up posters in strategic places across school, detailing how everyone can help pupils with ASDs
- To examine noise levels in the environment
- To consider arrangements at lunchtime and breaktimes.

School 4 is a primary school for pupils aged four to eleven years. It has recently become the resource base for seven youngsters with a diagnosis of ASDs from within the authority. Although pupils spend time at the resource base, there are also opportunities throughout the day for them to participate in mainstream activities. Staff are very much aware of the fact that the children with ASDs often become 'stressed out' during activities that involve the whole school, e.g. break, lunch, assembly, sports day etc. They also know of some children who would like to have a friend to talk to and turn to in times of need but who do not have the social skills to initiate this. Priorities of this school include:

- Introduce a buddy system at lunch and breaktimes
- Create a bank of 'relaxing resources' for pupils with ASDs
- Use more visual cues throughout the school – in particular visual timetables
- Place pupils with ASDs in a position of responsibility, e.g. a monitor to alleviate stress during transition times in the day
- Visit other schools in the authority to share best practice.

It is important that all targets set following an audit are SMART, i.e. specific, measurable, achievable, realistic and timed (ACCAC, 2000) and form part of the School Development Plan.

School access plan

Under the SENDA Act (DfES, 2001) all schools have a duty to produce a School Access Plan. This duty came into force in April 2003 when all schools were required to have a written plan covering an initial period of three years. The initial Plans covered the period from 1 April 2003 to 31 March 2006. To support this process, DfES has commissioned the Accessibility Planning Project (APP). The purpose of the project is to identify good practice in development, implementation and evaluation of accessibility plans and information from the project and guidance can be downloaded from www.dfes.gov.uk.

The plan can merge with existing plans but once it is in place it is the duty of the school to regularly review their plan by evaluating and revising where necessary and to implement the actions of the plan by allocating adequate resources.

The purpose of the School Action Plan is to:

- Increase the ways in which pupils with a disability can access the school curriculum
- Improve the physical environment of schools so that pupils with a disability can take full advantage of education and associated services
- Provide written information in a format that meets the needs of the individual and which takes account of the views expressed by pupils or parents regarding a preferred means of communication.

Schools can organize their plan using the following sub-headings:

- Target
- Strategy
- Resources
- Timescale
- Person Responsible
- Success Indicator

Short-, medium-and long-term plans can then be drawn up in relation to school buildings (exterior) and grounds, school buildings (interior), information and curriculum.

School buildings (interior and exterior) and grounds

For pupils with ASDs schools might consider:

- Access to a quiet area at break and lunchtimes, e.g. benches away from the main hub of activity
- Heating
- Lighting
- Noise levels/acoustics
- Access to a 'safe haven' indoors
- A place for possessions
- The level of safety and security that the environment offers
- Durable materials
- Seating and furniture
- Possible distractions
- Decoration – is the classroom over-stimulating?
- Signs and visual cues to help pupils move from one activity to another
- Arrangements in the dining room – lining up, making choices, seating, noise levels and other sensory issues.

Curriculum

Schools should consider:

- Language and communication issues, in particular their own language
- Audits of timetables to ascertain times/subjects that are likely to cause stress
- Use of visual timetables and other clues to assist learning, e.g. colour coding books, using picture symbols etc.
- Opportunities given to follow a special interest or access a safe haven
- Arrangements during non-contact time (lunch and breaks)
- Using senses to encourage understanding of different times and cultures
- Opportunities to generalize skills.

Information

Schools should think about:

- Information to pupils, especially pre-transition. Is it clearly written, unambiguous and visual?
- Access to information for reviews – pupil-friendly format, jargon-free
- Information to parents regarding school's provision for pupils with ASDs and support networks and other relevant contact details
- Production of accessible leaflet for parents and pupils about the school and arrangements/timetable for that year group
- Creating a resource bank of materials on ASDs for staff
- Information booklet explaining needs of pupils with ASDs for new staff and visitors to the school
- Ways in which awareness raising on ASDs can take place, e.g. staff meeting/carrying out an audit/notice boards/displays/INSET.

Disability equality duty

All primary and secondary schools maintained by a local education authority, and all local authorities themselves are covered by the Disability Equality Duty (DED). This means that alongside their existing duties, schools and local authorities have to take proactive steps to promote disability equality for pupils, employees and service users.

The general duty requires all public authorities to have due regard to the need to:

- Promote equality of opportunity
- Eliminate unlawful discrimination
- Promote positive attitudes towards disabled people
- Eliminate disability-related harassment
- Encourage disabled people's participation in public life
- Take steps to take into account people's disabilities, even where that involves more favourable treatment.

Certain listed public authorities are also covered by specific duties which set out certain measuring, action planning and reporting mechanisms that need to happen to meet the general duty. The most important requirement of the specific duties is to produce a Disability Equality Scheme (DES). Local Authorities in England and Wales and schools in England have had Schemes in place since December 2006. Schools in Wales have had Schemes in place since April 2007.

In their DES, schools must first state how they are meeting the general duties. For example, under the heading 'Eliminating Discrimination that is Unlawful' for pupils with an ASD these might include:

- Monitoring incidents of harassment and bullying and encouraging pupils to report incidents
- Investigating and addressing specific issues relating to ASDs in Circle Time, Assemblies and PSE lessons.
- Ensuring that information is available in accessible format.

Under the heading 'Promoting Positive Attitudes Towards Disabled People' consideration could be given to the following:

- Giving pupils roles of responsibility
- Ensuring that information about ASDs is represented in displays and learning materials.
- Using reading books and having books available in the library that show ASDs in a positive light.

It is a specific duty of the school to involve people with a disability in the development of the scheme. This can be done using focus groups, questionnaires, feedback slips, drop-in sessions and School Councils.

Schools should monitor the impact of their actions to ensure that progress is being made to meet the Disability Equality Duty. The action plan should be monitored in accordance with specified timescales. If any adverse impacts are noted then the Action Plan must be revised. Ideally an annual report should be produced which outlines the progress of the Disability Equality Scheme. The report should be circulated to the head teacher and governors and its findings used to improve the Disability Equality Scheme and future planning. A designated member of staff is to be responsible for monitoring and evaluation of the scheme.

The DED and the Access Plans are closely linked and can be well informed by using a self-evaluation tool.

 Extension activities

The following activities are intended to make participants reflect upon their own practice in relation to individuals with ASDs. The activities also encourage them to examine the school environment in terms of 'ASD-friendliness'. Figure 1.3 – How ASD-Friendly Are You? could be distributed to provoke discussion and some self-reflection prior to one of these activities.

- Ask participants to complete the checklist (Figure 12.1) to consider where their school is in relation to these questions. After some debate (at your discretion), show the PowerPoint slides of case study schools' targets. These will help to demonstrate that issues will need to be addressed in a bite-sized realistic way. Let participants know

Continued

that you understand that they have to meet the needs of a range of pupils but explain that focusing on one group can often have a positive knock-on effect for other pupils. Ask them to spend fifteen minutes writing three/four targets that would be achievable in the short term.

- Ask participants to bring a copy of their School's Access and Inclusion Plan and DES to the training event. Is there evidence that both are meeting or even considering the needs of pupils with ASDs? Use the PowerPoint slides as an aide-mémoire to prompt discussion.

PowerPoint presentation

The slides can be used to complete the activities. It is important for facilitators to emphasize that self-evaluation can be used effectively to highlight priorities for pupils with ASDs. Also it is a useful exercise to undertake to inform the content of the School Access and Inclusion Plan and the school's response to the Disability Equality Duty. ASDs is sometimes referred to as 'the hidden disability' and may not always be considered as fully as physical or sensory disabilities.

Recommended reading

The recommended reading for this section focuses on government legislation and initiatives and will help the reader to have a better understanding of the value of audit and also of issues relating to the DED. We highly recommend that readers visit the Disability Rights Commission's Website to fully familiarize themselves with the duties placed on schools, especially as ASDs is often referred to as 'the hidden disability'. Many of the texts are available on the internet and so website addresses have been provided. The ASD *Good Practice Guidance* is extremely useful and contains detailed checklists for use in both schools and local authorities.

DfES (2002) *Autistic Spectrum Disorders: Good Practice Guidance,* Nottingham:DfES.
Disability Rights Commission (2006) *The Disability Equality Duty. What Does it Mean for Schools in England and Wales?* http://www.drc-gb.org/PDF/DED%20schools%20flyer.pdf
Implementation Review Unit (2007) *IRU Statement on SEN and Disability – Meeting Need, Minimising Bureaucracy* – www.teachernet.gov.uk
National Initiative for Autism: Screening and Assessment (NIASA) (2003) *NAP-C: Plan for the Identification, Assessment and Diagnosis of Children with ASDs.* London: National Autistic Society.
Ofsted/DfEs (2005) *A New Relationship with Schools: Improving Performance through School Self Evaluation.* Available from www.teachernet.gov.uk

Useful websites

www.dotheduty.org
www.teachernet.gov.uk/wholeschool/sen
www.learning.wales.gov.uk
www.dfes.gov.uk/sen
www.deni.gov.uk
www.scotland.gov.uk

 Go to the accompanying CD-Rom for the full selection of slides that accompany this section and remember you can also access detailed speaker notes to use with each slide.

Figure 12.1 Checklist for Schools

TARGET	Y	N	Any Action?
Is there someone in school with experience of and responsibility for ASDs?			
Are all staff aware of the implications of the Triad of Impairments, i.e. how much awareness raising has taken place?			
Is there a resource bank of materials on ASDs?			
Are activities and timetables differentiated to meet the needs of pupils with ASDs?			
Are there opportunities to generalize skills?			
Has the school environment been modified to take account of sensory issues?			
How does the school share information with parents?			
Is there good communication between all agencies involved with the pupil?			
Are there opportunities to share best practice on ASDs with other schools?			
Are staff aware of the impact of sensory and social issues upon behaviour?			
Are structures in place to warn pupils with ASDs about a possible changes in routine/activity?			
Are pupils with ASDs given time to follow a special interest and is a 'safe haven' available during times of stress?			
Does the school provide opportunities for pupils with ASDs to develop their social skills?			
Are new staff and visitors given information on ASDs and the school's policy and procedure?			

The Autism Inclusion Toolkit, SAGE, 2008 © Maggie Bowen and Lynn Plimley

Section 12:

CARRYING OUT A SCHOOL AUDIT AND PLANNING FOR ACCESS AND INCLUSION

1

Why is Self-Evaluation Important?

Self-evaluation helps schools to look at their evidence base for a set of targets in order to improve provision

2

Pupils with ASDs
Points to Consider in Self-Evaluation

- Is there someone in school with experience of and responsibility for ASDs?

- Are all staff aware of the educational implications of the Triad of Impairment, i.e how much awareness raising has taken place?

- Are timetables and activities differentiated to meet the needs of pupils with ASDs

3

ASDs Issues continued

- Does the school provide opportunities for skills to be generalized?

- Has the environment been modified to take account of sensory issues?

- How does the school share information with parents?

- Is there good communication between all agencies/people involved with pupils?

4

ASDs Issues continued

- Are there opportunities to share best practice with other schools?

- Are staff aware of the impact of social issues and sensory issues on behaviour?

- Are structures in place to warn about possible changes in routines/activities?

- Are pupils allowed time to follow a special interest?

5

ASDs Issues continued

- Does the school provide opportunities for pupils to develop their social skills?

- Are new staff and visitors given information on ASDs and the school's policy and procedure?

- Are procedures in place at break and lunchtimes to avoid 'melt down' and possible bullying?

6

Priorities for School 1

- Continue to modify the school environment to take account of sensory issues

- Staff will share information on ASDs in a formal way when they attend a training event

- There will be an up–to–date bank of resources on ASDs

- The school will develop a specific policy

7

Priorities for School 2

- To develop a policy document with outside agencies and the voluntary sector

- Pupils with ASDs will be more involved in decision making

- Time will be allocated to follow a special interest

- A section of the library will be used as a 'safe haven'

8

Priorities for School 3

- To develop a policy document with outside agencies
- To have a whole school training day on ASDs
- To create a resource bank of materials
- To put posters up in strategic places in school explaining how everyone can help pupils with ASDs
- To examine noise levels in the environment
- To consider arrangements at break and lunchtimes

9

Priorities for School 4

- Introduce a buddy system at break and lunchtimes
- Create a bank of 'relaxing' resources for pupils with ASDs
- Use more visual cues throughout the school- visual timetables for everyone!
- Place pupils with ASDs in position of responsibility, e.g. a monitor during transition times to alleviate stress
- SENCo to visit other schools in the authority to examine best practice

10

School Access and Inclusion Plan and Disability Equality Duty

Evidence from the Self-evaluation Tool can be used to inform the School's Access and Inclusion Plan and provide evidence that duties are being met under the Disability Equality Duty (Disability Rights Commission, 2006)

11

School Environment

- Is there access to a quiet area at break and lunchtimes away from the main hub of activity?
- Have you considered heating, lighting, noise levels in and around school?
- Is there a safe haven indoors?
- What safety and security does the environment offer?

12

School Environment continued

- Are resources/materials durable and how is seating and furniture arranged ?
- How are classrooms/corridors decorated-are they over-stimulating?
- Are signs and visual cues in place to help pupils move around school and from activity to activity with ease?
- What issues need addressing in the hall at dinner times and Assembly?

13

Curriculum
Points to Consider

- Language and communication
- Audits of timetables to ascertain times/subjects that are likely to cause stress
- Use of visual timetables and other clues to assist learning, e.g. colour coded-books, use of picture symbols

14

Curriculum
Points to Consider continued

- Opportunities are provided to follow a special interest
- There is access to a 'safe haven'
- Arrangements at break and lunchtimes
- The use of sensory experiences to understand different times and cultures
- There are opportunities to generalize skills

15

Information
Points to Consider

- Information given to pupils especially pre transition is clearly written, unambiguous and visual
- Information for reviews is written in friendly format and is jargon-free
- Parents have information about the school's provision for pupils with ASDs and a list of relevant support groups and contacts

16

Information Points to Consider continued	Disability Equality Duty
• Production of accessible leaflets for parents and pupils about the school's arrangements/timetable for that year group • There is a resource bank of materials on ASD for staff • Information on ASDs is available to new staff and visitors to the school • Awareness-raising takes place in a number of ways	Examine your school's plan. Are the needs of pupils with ASDs addressed under the duties? Remember ASDs is a disability and so the school has a legal obligation to consider and meet the needs of pupils with ASDs.
17	18

Useful Organizations

National Groups

Autism Cymru, Wales' national charity for autism.
National Office
6 Great Darkgate Street
Aberystwyth
Ceredigion
SY23 1DE
Tel: 01978 853841
Email: maggie@autismcymru.org
Website: www.awares.org

Autism Northern Ireland (PAPA)
Donard
Knockbracken Healthcare Park
Saintfield
Belfast
BT8 8BH
Tel: 0208 9040 1729
Email: info@autismni.org
Website: www.autismni.org

The Scottish Society for Autism
Head Office
Hilton House
Alloa Business Park
Whins Road
Alloa FK10 3SA
Tel: 01259 720044
Email: autism@autism-in-scotland.org.uk
Website: www.autism-in-scotland.org.uk

The Irish Society for Autism
Unity Building,
16/17, Lower O'Connell Street,
Dublin, 1
Email: autism@isa.iol.ie
Website: http://www.iol.ie/~isa1/

National Autistic Society
393 City Road
London EC1V 1NE

Tel: 020 7833 2299 for general enquiries
Helpline: 0845 070 4004
Parent to Parent support line: 0800 9 520 520
Email: nas@nas.org.uk
Website: www.nas.org.uk

Association of Head Teachers of Autistic Children and Adults (AHTACA)
1 Aston Road, Ealing, London W5 2RL
Tel: 020 8998 2700

College of Speech and Language Therapists
7 Bath Place, Rivington Street, London EC21 3DR
Tel: 020 7613 3855

Education

For free copies of *The Special Educational Needs Code of Practice* and the useful booklet *Special Educational Needs (SEN): A Guide for Parents and Carers*, contact:

The Publications Department
The Department of Education and Skills
P.O. Box 5050
Sherwood Park
Annersley
Nottingham
NG15 ODJ
Tel: 0845 6022260
Email: dfes@prolog.uk.com
Website: www.dfes.gov.uk/sen

IPSEA offers independent, free advice on the duties of local authorities for the educational needs of children with SEN:
Independent Panel for Special Educational Advice (IPSEA)
6 Carlow Mews
Woodbridge
Suffolk
IP12 1EA

Advice Line (England and Wales): 0800 018 4016
(Scotland): 0131 454 0082
(Northern Ireland): 01232 705654
Website: www.ipsea.org.uk

Centre for Studies on Inclusive Education (CSIE) – for information and advice on educating children with SEN in mainstream schools:
New Redland
Frenchay Campus
Coldharbour Lane
Bristol
BS16 1QU
Tel: 0117 344 4007
Fax: 0117 344 4005
Website: www.inclusion.org.uk

Turner Library–SEN Information Service
Whitefield Schools and Centre, Macdonald Road, Walthamstow,
London E17 4AZ
Tel: 020 8531 8703
Email : lib@whitefield.org.uk

Financial

Disability Alliance – campaigns for disabled people and their families and can offer benefits entitlement advice:
Universal House
88–94 Wentworth Street
London E1 7SA
Tel: 020 7247 8776
Fax: 020 7247 8765
Website: www.disabilityalliance.org

Disability Benefit Enquiry Line – for benefits advice: contact Freephone 0800 882200

Disability Living Allowance Advice Line: contact 08457 123456 (local rate)

Practical

RADAR (The Royal Association for Disability and Rehabilitation) – campaigns and provides information on disability issues. Radar keys unlock public toilets for the disabled and are a boon for parents out and about with an autistic child of the opposite gender from themselves:
12 City Forum
250 City Road
London EC1V 8AF
Tel: 020 7250 3222
Fax: 020 7250 0212
Minicom: 020 7250 4119
Email: radar@radar.org.uk
Website: www.mencap.org.uk

Legal

The Children's Legal Centre
University of Essex
Wivenhoe Park
Colchester CO4 3FQ
An independent, national charity concerned with law and policy affecting children and young people. It operates an Education Law and Advocacy Unit and its lawyers and barristers provide free legal advice on all aspects of education law. Contact: 0845 120 2966

References

ACCAC (2000) *A Structure for Successs. Guidance on National Curriculum and Autistic Spectrum Disorders*. Birmingham: ACCAC.

Attfield, E. and Morgan, S.H. (2006) *Living with Autistic Spectrum Disorders*. London: Paul Chapman/ Sage Publications.

Audit Scotland/HMIe (2003) *Moving to Mainstream. The Inclusion of Pupils with Special Educational Needs in Mainstream Schools. Main Report*. Edinburgh: Auditor General.

Ayres, A.J. (1979) *Sensory Integration and the Child*. Los Angeles: Western Psychological Services.

Bache, K., Daniels, E., Hewison, S. and Young, P. (2004) *Guidelines for Working with Children with ASDs at Foundation Phase or KS1*, www.southglos.gov.uk

Baird, G., Simonoff, E., Pickles, A. et al. (2006) 'Prevalence of disorders of the autism spectrum in a population cohort of children in South Thames: the Special Needs and Autism Project (SNAP)', *Lancet*, 368: 210–15.

Baron-Cohen, S., Leslie, A.M. and Frith, U. (1985) 'Does the autistic child have a theory of mind', *Cognition*, 21 (10): 37–46.

Baron-Cohen, S. (2003) *The Essential Difference*. London: Penguin

Bogdashina, O. (2003) *Sensory Perceptual Issues in Autism and Asperger Syndrome Different Sensory Experiences Different Perceptual Worlds*. London: Jessica Kingsley Publishers.

Bondy, A and Frost, L. (1994) 'The Delaware Autistic Program,' in S.L. Harris and J.S. Handleman (eds), *Preschool Education Programs for Children with Autism*. Austin, TX: Pro-Ed.

Betts, S.W., Betts, D.E. and Gerber-Eckard, L.N. (2007) *Asperger Syndrome in the Inclusive Classroom. Advice and Strategies for Teachers*. London: Jessica Kingsley.

Chara, K.A., Chara, P.J. with Chara, C. (2004) *Sensory Smarts: A Book for Kids with ADHD or Autism Spectrum Disorders Struggling with Sensory Integration Problems*. London: Jessica Kingsley.

Cook, L.L. and Stowe, S. (2003) *Talk given on Nottingham Inclusion Support Service at Distance Education (ASD) weekend*, School of Education, University of Birmingham.

Cumine, V. Leach, J. and Stevenson, G. (1998) *Asperger Syndrome – A Practical Guide for Teachers*. London: David Fulton Publishers Ltd.

Dawson, G. and Osterling, J. (1997) 'Early intervention in autism', in M. Guralnick (ed), *The Effectiveness of Early Intervention*. Baltimore, MD: Brookes.

Department for Education and Skills (DfES) (1989) *The Children Act*. http://www.dfes.gov.uk/publications/childrenactreport/

Department for Education and Skills (DfES)(2001) *The Code of Practice for Special Educational Needs*. Nottingham: DfES Publications.

Department for Education and Skills (DfES) (2001) *Special Educational Needs and Disability Act (SENDA)*. London: HMSO.

Department for Education and Skills/Department of Health (DfES) (2002) *Autistic Spectrum Disorders: Good Practice Guidance*. Nottingham: DfES.

Department for Education and Skills (DfES) *ASD Good Practice Guidance – Early Years Examples*. http://www.teachernet.gov.uk (accessed 04/06/07)

Department for Education and Skills (2002) *SEN Toolkit*. www.dfes.gov.uk/sen

Department for Education and Skills (2003) *Every Child Matters*. www.everychildmatters.gov.uk (accessed 04/06/07)

Department for Education and Skills (2005) *Education Act*. http://www.opsi.gov.uk/acts/acts2005/20050018.htm

Department of Education, Northern Ireland (2003) *Autistic Spectrum Disorders – a Guide to Classroom Practice.* Belfast: DENI.

DENI (2005) *Special educational needs and disability order (SENDO).* http://www.deni.gov.uk/index/7-special_educational_needs_pg/special_needs-legislation_pg/special_educational_needs-legislation_pg.htm (accessed 04/06/07)

Department of Work and Pensions (1995) *The Disability Discrimination Act.* London: HMSO. http://www.direct.gov.uk/en/DisabledPeople/RightsAndObligations/DisabilityRights/DG_4001068

Department of Work and Pensions (2005) *The Disability Discrimination Act.* http://www.opsi.gov.uk/ACTS/acts2005/20050013.htm

Disability Rights Commission (2006) *The Disability Equality Duty. What does it Mean for Schools in England and Wales?* http://www.drc-gb.org/PDF/DED%20schools%20flyer.pdf

Emerson, E. (2001) *Challenging Behaviour: Analysis and Intervention in People with Severe Intellectual Disabilities.* Cambridge: Cambridge University Press.

Eduction and Training Inspectorate, Northern Ireland (ETINI) (2002) *Autistic Spectrum Disorders – a Guide to Classroom Practice.* http://www.etini.gov.uk/asd_classroom_practice.pdf (accessed 04/06/07)

Frith, U. (1989) *Autism: Explaining the Enigma.* Oxford: Blackwell.

Frith, U. and Happe, F. (1994) 'Autism – beyond a theory of mind', *Cognition*, 50(1-3): 115–32.

Ganz, J. B. and Simpson, R. L. (2004) 'Effects on communicative requesting and speech development of the picture exchange communication system in children with characteristics of autism', *Journal of Autism and Developmental Disorders*, 34(4): 395–409.

Gold, D. (1999) 'Friendship, leisure and support: The purposes of "Circles of Friends" of Young People', *Journal of Leisurability*, 26(3). http://www.lin.ca/resource/html/Vol26/V26N3A2.htm

Grandin, T. (1995) 'How people with autism think' in E. Schopler and G.B. Mesibov (eds), *Learning and Cognition in Autism.* New York: Plenum Press.

Grandin, T. (1996) *Thinking in Pictures and Other Reports From My Life with Autism.* California: Vintage Press.

Grandin, T. (1999) *Genius May be an Abnormality: Educating Students with Asperger Syndrome and High Functioning Autism.* Paper presented during Autism 99 (Conference on the Internet), www.autism99.

Gray, A.C. (1994) *Social Stories.* Arlington, TX: Future Horizons.

Gray, A.C. (2000) *The New Social Story Book: Illustrated edition.* Arlington, TX: Future Horizons.

Gray, A.C. and Leigh White, A. (eds) (2002) *My Social Stories Book.* Arlington, TX: Future Horizons.

Hart, R. (1992) *Children's Participation – From Tokenism to Citizenship.* London: UNICEF International Child Development Centre.

Haddon, M. (2003) *The Curious Incident of the Dog in the Night Time,* (Adult Version). London: Vintage UK.

Haddon, M. (2004) *The Curious Incident of the Dog in the Night Time,* (Children's Version). London: Random House Children's Books (UK).

Her Majesty's Inspectorate for Education (2006) *Education for Pupils with Autism Spectrum Disorders Report.* http://www.hmie.gov.uk/documents/publication/epasd.pdf (accessed 04/06/07)

Hinder, S. (2004) 'Lecture on sensory differences in people with ASD', Paper presented at *Good Autism Practice Journal Conference, Harrogate.*

Hoopmann, K. (2001) *The Blue Bottle Mystery.* London: Jessica Kingsley Publications.

Humphreys, S. (2005) *Autism and Architecture.* www.autismlondon.org.uk/pdf-files/bulletin_feb-mar_2005.pdf

Implementation Review Unit (2007) *IRU Statement on SEN and Disability – Meeting Need, Minimising Bureaucracy.* www.teachernet.gov.uk

Jackson, L. (2002) *Freaks, Geeks and Asperger Syndrome.* London: Jessica Kingsley Publishers.

Jackson, N. (2002) *Standing Down Falling Up, Asperger Syndrome from the Inside Out.* Bristol: Lucky Duck Publishing.

Jones, V. (2004) 'The efficacy of the Picture Exchange Communication System (PECS) in developing spontaneous communication', *Good Autism Practice*, 5(2): 42–7.

Jordan, R.R. (1999) *Autistic Spectrum Disorders – An Introductory Handbook for Practitioners.* London: David Fulton.

Jordan, R., Jones, G. and Murray, D. (1998) *Educational Interventions for Children with Autism: A Literature Review of Recent and Current Research, Report 77.* Sudbury: DfEE.

Jordan, R., Jones, G. and Morgan, S.H. (2001) *A Guide to Services for Children with Autistic Spectrum Disorders for Commissioners and Providers.* London: Mental Health Foundation.

Kanner, L. (1943) 'Autistic disturbances of effective contact', *Nervous Child*, 2: 217–50.

Kluth, P. (2003) *You're Gonna Love this Kid.* Maryland: Paul H. Brookes.

La Vigna, G.W. and Donnellan, A.M. (1986) *Alternatives to Punishment: Solving Behavior Problems with Non-aversive Strategies.* New York. Irvington Publishers.

Latiff, A. (2006) *Diagnostic Trends in the SouthWales Valleys (not yet published)*

Lawson, W. (2000) *A Life through Glass.* London: Jessica Kingsley Publishers.

Lawson, W. (2001) *Understanding and Working with the Spectrum of Autism.* London: Jessica Kingsley Publishers.

Lee O'Neil, J.(1999) *Through the Eyes of Aliens. A Book About Autistic People.* London: Jessica Kingsley Publishers.

Mesibov, G., Shea, V. and Schopler, E. (2004) *The TEACCH Approach to Autism Spectrum Disorders.* New York: Plenum Press.

Mitchell, C. (2005) *Glass Half Empty. Glass Half Full. How Asperger's Syndrome Changed My Life.* London: Paul Chapman Publishing/Lucky Duck Books.

Mitchell, C. (2007) *Managing Transition to Higher Education for Students with Asperger's Syndrome.* Paper presented at 'Shaping the Future Conference', NEWI, London, 27 June.

Myles, Brenda Smith and Southwick, J. (2001) *Asperger Syndrome and Sensory Issues:Practical Solutions for Making Sense of the Real World.* Shawnee Mission, Kansas: Autism Asperger Publishing Company.

National Initiative for Autism: Screening and Assessment (NIASA) (2003) *NAP-C: Plan for the Identification, Assessment and Diagnosis of Children with ASDs.* London: National Autistic Society.

Ofsted/DfEs (2005) *A New Relationship with Schools: Improving Performance through School Self Evaluation.* Available from www.teachernet.gov.uk

Ozonoff, S., Pennington, B.F. and Rogers, S.J. (1991) 'Executive function deficits in high functioning autistic individuals – relationship to theory of mind', *Journal of Child Psychology and Psychiatry and Allied Disciplines*, 32(7): 1081–122.

Parents and Professionals Autism (PAPA) Department of Education, Department of Education and Science, NI (2003) *Autistic spectrum disorder – a Teacher's Toolkit CD-ROM.*

Pavey, B. (2007) *The Dyslexia Friendly Primary School.* London: Paul Chapman/Sage Publications.

Plimley, L.A. (2004) 'Analysis of a student task to create an autism-friendly living environment', *Good Autism Practice (GAP) Journal*, 5(2): 35–41.

Plimley, L.A. (2007) *A review of quality of life issues and people with autism spectrum disorders.* http://www.blackwell-synergy.com/doi/abs/10.1111/j.1468-3156.2007.00448.x

Plimley, L.A. and Bowen, M. (2006a) *Autistic Spectrum Disorders in the Secondary School.* London: Paul Chapman/Sage Publications.

Plimley, L.A. and Bowen, M. (2006b) *Supporting Pupils with Autistic Spectrum Disorders.* London: Paul Chapman/Sage Publications.

Plimley, L.A. and Bowen, M. (2007) *Social Skills and Autistic Spectrum Disorders.* London: Paul Chapman/Sage Publications.

Plimley, L.A., Bowen, M. and Morgan, H. (2007) *ASDs in the Early Years.* London: Paul Chapman/Sage Publications.

Premack, D. and Woodruff, G. (1978) 'Does the chimpanzee have a theory of mind ?', *Behavioural and Brain Sciences*, 1(4): 515–26.

Presland, J. (1989) *Action Record for Problem Behaviour.* Kidderminster: British Institute of Mental Handicap.

Rajendran, G. and Mitchell, P. (2007) 'Cognitive theories of autism', *Developmental Review*, 27(2): 224–60.

Rinaldi, W. (1993) *The Social Use of Language Programme.* Windsor: NFER.

Rowe, C. (1999) 'Do Social Stories benefit children with autism in mainstream primary school?', *British Journal of Special Education*, 26(1): 12–14.

Sainsbury, C. (2000) *Martian in the Playground.* London: Lucky Duck/Paul Chapman.

Schopler, E. and Mesibov, G. (1995) 'Structured teaching in the TEACCH approach', in E. Schopler and G. Mesibov (eds), *Learning and Cognition in Autism.* New York: Plenum Press.

Treseder, P. (1997) *Empowering Childen and Young People Training Manual: Promoting Involvement in Decision Making.* London: Children's Rights Office/ Save the Children.

United Nations (1991) *Rights of the Child.* http://www.unhchr.ch/html/menu6/2/fs10.htm

Waltz, M. (2005) *Metaphors of Autism and Autism as a Metaphor.* www.interdisciplinary.net/mso/hid/hid2/hid03s11a.htm

Welsh Assembly Government (2002) *Handbook of Good Practice for Children with Special Educational Needs.* Cardiff: Welsh Assembly Government.

Welsh Assembly Government (2002) *Special Needs Code of Practice for Wales.* Cardiff: Welsh Assembly Government.

Welsh Assembly Government Participation Consortium (2004) *Children and Young People's Participation: Working Towards a Definition.* A discussion paper.

Welsh Assembly Government (2007) *Rights to Action. Implementing Children and Young People's Rights in Wales.*

Welsh Assembly Government (2007) *Strategic Action Plan for Wales – ASDs.* (Consultation Document).

West Midlands Regional Co-ordination Project (2001) *Report on Autistic Spectrum Disorders.* http://www.westmidlandsrcp.org.uk/PDFs/Report%20on%20Autistic%20Spectrum% 20Disorders%20-%20Foreword01.pdf (accessed 04/06/07)

Whitaker, P. (2001) *Challenging behaviour and autism. Making Sense – Making Progress.* London: National Autistic Society.

Whitaker, P., Barratt, P., Joy, H., Potter, M. and Thomas, G. (1998) 'Children with autism and peer support using "Circle of Friends"', *British Journal of Special Education,* 25(2): 60–4.

Whitehurst, T. (2006) 'The impact of building design on children with autistic spectrum disorders', *Good Autism Practice (GAP) Journal,* 7(1): 31–8.

Williams, D. (1992) *Nobody, Nowhere.* New York: Time Books.

Williams, D. (1996) *Autism an Inside-out Approach.* London: Jessica Kingsley Publishers.

Williams, D. (1998) *Autism and Sensing.* London: Jessica Kingsley Publishers.

Wing, L. (1981) Asperger's syndrome: A clinical account, *Psychological Medicine,* 11(1): 115–30.

Wing, L. (1988) 'The continuum of autistic disorders' in E. Schopler and G.M. Mesibov (eds), *Diagnosis and Assessment In Autism.* New York: Plenum. pp. 91–110.

Wing, L. (1996) *The Autistic Spectrum.* London: Constable.

Zarkowska, E. and Clements J. (1994) *Problem Behaviour and People with Severe Learning Difficulties.* London: Chapman and Hall.

Index